DK EYE ~~WITNESS~~ ~~TRAVEL~~ EL

W9-AEG-096

TOP 10
MUNICH

ELFI LEDIG

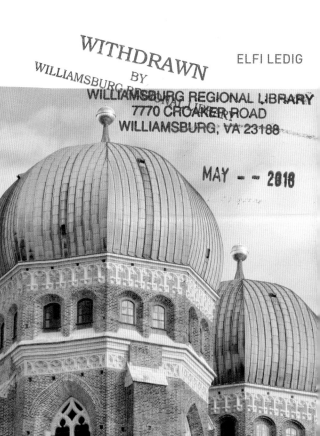

Penguin Random House

Top 10 Munich Highlights

The Top 10 of Everything

CONTENTS

Munich Area by Area

Streetsmart

Within each Top 10 list in this book, no hierarchy of quality or popularity is implied. All 10 are, in the editor's opinion, of roughly equal merit.

Front cover and spine
The Chinesischer Turm in the Englischer Garten
Back cover
Schloss Nymphenburg
Title page *The towers of the Frauenkirche*

Welcome to
Munich

With its blue-and-white skies, Baroque churches, and an almost Mediterranean outlook, it's hardly surprising that the state capital of Bavaria is such a hotspot for tourists. It welcomes around 7 million foreign visitors each year and is one of the most liveable metropolises in the world. With Eyewitness Top 10 Munich, it's yours to explore.

Munich is a city of almost 1.5 million inhabitants, and one look at its many squares filled with bustling cafés will tell you it's a city that enjoys the good life. Locals are spoilt for choice when it comes to the number of green spaces in which to unwind, including the **Englischer Garten** and the Isar river meadows. For fans of sport and the great outdoors, the **Olympiapark** is a top city destination; the Upper Bavarian **lakes** and nearby **Alps** also lie within easy reach.

Ludwig I transformed Munich into his vision of "Athens on the Isar". Today, the city is blessed with more art institutions than ever, most of which can be found in the **museum quarter**. This is where the city's three **Pinakotheken** (art museums) are located, along with its two universities. Just as importantly, Munich is Germany's undisputed capital of beer, thanks to the brewing expertise of the monks who settled on the Isar back in the 13th century. It plays host to the annual **Oktoberfest** and to countless **beer gardens**.

Whether you're visiting for the weekend or a longer stay, our Top 10 travel guide brings you the best that Munich has to offer – from its **Deutsches Museum** of science and **BMW Welt** right through to the fairy-tale **Neuschwanstein** castle. It's also jam-packed with useful tips, plus nine easy-to-follow itineraries, designed to help you get the most out of your visit. Add inspiring photography and detailed maps, and you've got the essential pocket-sized travel companion. **Enjoy the book, and enjoy Munich.**

Clockwise from top: **Staatstheater am Gärtnerplatz; Hofbräuhaus; Olympiapark; Schloss Nymphenburg; a Residenz lion; Oktoberfest ride**

Exploring Munich

Whether it's sightseeing, shopping or simply savouring the atmosphere, Munich has everything you're looking for and more. The old town and the Englischer Garten can be done in just a couple of days, while those with more time to spare can also add Nymphenburg and Olympiapark to the list. These itineraries are designed to help you pack in as many of the city's highlights as possible.

The mushroom water fountains by Frauenkirche – a popular place to cool off in summer.

Key

— Two-day itinerary

— Four-day itinerary

Two Days in Munich

Day ❶

MORNING

Start the day at Frauenkirche (see pp14–15). Be sure to make your way to Marienplatz (see pp12–13) by 11am to experience the famous Glockenspiel chiming clock. Next, head to Peterskirche (see pp78–9) and climb the tower for a breathtaking view of the city. Round off the morning with a stroll at Viktualienmarkt (see p80).

AFTERNOON

Visit St-Jakobs-Platz to take in the synagogue and the Münchner Stadtmuseum (see p80) before heading over to Asamkirche (see p80–81). From here, amble across Marienhof to take in the Staatsoper (see p89) and Residenz (see pp16–17).

Day ❷

MORNING

Make a start at Odeonsplatz, where you'll find the Theatinerkirche and Feldherrnhalle (see pp90–91), before

making a turn into the Hofgarten. Passing through the garden, you'll reach the Haus der Kunst museum (see p104), and outside you'll find the famous Eisbach surfers navigating the icy waters of the stream.

AFTERNOON

Spend the afternoon in the Munich's main park, the Englischer Garten (see pp22–3), and make a pit stop at the Chinesischer Turm or Seehaus.

Four Days in Munich

Day ❶

MORNING

Start in Marienplatz (see pp12–13) and take in everything the area has to offer: Viktualienmarkt (see p80), Sendlinger Straße and Kaufinger Straße, all the way to the Frauenkirche (see pp14–15).

AFTERNOON

Odeonsplatz is where you'll find the Feldherrnhalle and even get the opportunity to peek inside the Theatinerkirche (see p91). Make your

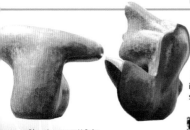

Two-Piece Reclining Figure: Points is a bronze monumental sculpture created in 1969–70 by English sculptor Henry Moore. It is one of the most important of the sculptures surrounding the Pinakotheken.

The Lenbachhaus once belonged to painter Franz von Lenbach and is now home to a collection of works by the "Blue Rider" group.

way to the **Hofgarten** and take a tour of the **Residenz** *(see pp16–17)*.

Day ❷
MORNING
Start with a stroll in the **Englischer Garten** *(see pp22–3)*, then head to **Münchner Freiheit** via Feilitzsch-straße. Take the U3 towards Olympia-park or walk down Leopoldstraße and Ludwigstraße, passing *Walking Man (see p104)*, the Siegestor and **Bayerische Staatsbibliothek** *(see p103)*.
AFTERNOON
Once you reach Odeonsplatz, take the U3 as far as Olympiazentrum. Here you can visit **BMW Welt** and the **BMW Museum** *(see p128–9)*, and take in the fascinating architecture of **Olympiapark** *(see pp32–3)*.

Day ❸
MORNING
Today's a day for museums, starting at **Königsplatz,** where you're spoilt

for choice with the **Glyptothek,** **Staatliche Antikensammlungen** and Lenbachhaus *(see p97)*, the three **Pinakotheken** *(see p18–21)*, **Museum Brandhorst** *(see p98)* and the **Ägyptisches Museum** *(see p98)*.
AFTERNOON
Take bus 100 to **Ostbahnhof** and stroll through **Haidhausen** *(see p113)* with its vast selection of shops and public spaces. Next, head past **Gasteig** *(see p112)* to reach the **Deutsches Museum** *(see pp26–9)*.

Day ❹
Today is all about **Schloss Nymphenburg** *(see pp30–31)* , a historic palace with extensive grounds and pavilions. When you're ready for a break, the **Schlosscafé im Palmenhaus** *(see p130)* is a great place to refuel. Afterwards, stop in at the **Botanischer Garten** *(see p127)* and see the day out in the nearby **Hirschgarten** *(see p128)*.

Top 10 Munich Highlights

Dramatically sited Neuschwanstein, a fairy-tale castle set amid the stunning Bavarian landscape

🔟 Munich Highlights

Munich is Germany's third-largest city, and before the fall of the Berlin Wall it was dubbed the "unofficial capital of the country". Not only does it boast historical buildings, museums filled with treasures, and a thriving cultural landscape, it also offers an abundance of recreational activities and a laid-back atmosphere.

① Around Marienplatz

Marienplatz is home to the Neues Rathaus and its famous Glockenspiel chiming clock (see pp12–13).

Frauenkirche ②

The domes of this Gothic cathedral – also known as the Münchner Dom – became the model for Baroque onion domes throughout Bavaria (see pp14–15).

③ Residenz

Dating back to 1385, the Residenz has been expanded by various wings and courtyards over the centuries (see pp16–17).

Pinakotheken ④

The three Pinakotheken can be found in the museum quarter. The oldest of these, the Alte Pinakothek (1836) houses priceless works of art (see pp18–21).

⑤ Englischer Garten

Munich's main green space is one of the largest inner-city parks in the world and a popular spot to unwind for locals and tourists alike (see pp22–23).

LANDSHUTER ALLEE
EBENAU
LEONROD-PLATZ
LEONRODSTR.
DACHAUER STR.
ACKERMANNK
⑧ Olympiasee
PLATZ DER FREIHEIT
⑦
3 km (2 miles)
NYMPHENBURGER STRASSE
MARSFELD
MARS-PLATZ MARSS
ARNULFSTRASSE
LANDSBERGER STRASSE
SCHWANTHALER-HÖHE
THERESIENHÖHE
⑨ Theresienwiese
BAVARIARING

Deutsches Museum ⑥

Pulling in more than 1.5 million visitors every year, this institution is the world's oldest and largest museum of science and technology and not to be missed *(see pp26–29)*.

⑦ Schloss Nymphenburg

This summer palace from 1664 was once situated outside the city. Its extensive grounds make it a green oasis in west Munich *(see pp30–31)*.

Around Munich ⑦

⑧ Olympiapark

The tent-style construction of the Olympic Stadium (1972) was an innovative feat of architecture when it was first built and it's still worth a visit today *(see pp32–3)*.

⑨ Oktoberfest

Millions of visitors flock to the largest beer festival in the world *(see pp34–5)*.

Neuschwanstein ⑩

Ludwig II's most famous castle was inspired by his admiration for Wagner operas *(see pp36–37)*.

TOP10 ⭐ Around Marienplatz

Marienplatz has been the heart of Munich for centuries and is still the most popular place in the city to meet up or start a walking tour. The square is dominated by the Neues Rathaus (New Town Hall), which serves as a backdrop to the Mariensäule (Column of the Virgin Mary) and Fischbrunnen (Fish Fountain). Head west of the square to reach the start of the pedestrian zone, north for Weinstraße and Theatiner-straße, east for the Isartor gate and Maximilianstraße, and south to reach Viktualienmarkt.

Neues Rathaus ②
The Neo-Gothic town hall **(right)** was built between 1867 and 1909. At the top of the tower sits the city mascot, the Münchner Kindl (Munich Child), while the famous Glockenspiel chiming clock show takes place daily in its alcoves (see p79).

③ Marienhof and Dallmayr
Behind the town hall lies Marienhof, a green oasis of recreation and culture. The impressive yellow-and-white façade on the right belongs to the renowned foodie paradise of Dallmayr (see p93).

① Altes Rathaus
This Gothic building dating back to 1470 **(above)** is situated in the eastern corner of Marienplatz and features both a grand hall and a tower (formerly the gateway to the city). This tower is now home to the toy museum (see p79).

④ Peterskirche
Munich's oldest parish church sits atop the highest point in the old town. Its Renaissance tower, known as "Alter Peter" (Old Pete), is one of the city's best-known landmarks (see p44 and pp78–9).

⑤ Odeonsplatz
A wander around Odeonsplatz shows why Munich is sometimes called "Italy's northern-most city". The square is bordered by the Italianate, late Baroque Theatinerkirche, the Residenz, the Hofgarten and its archways, and Feldherrnhalle **(left)**, built in 1844 by Friedrich von Gärtner, who drew inspiration from the Florentine Loggia dei Lanzi (see p91).

6 Viktualienmarkt

This daily food market originated in 1807, and a stroll through its 140 stalls is a real must. The southernmost end is home to Der Pschorr and the Schrannenhalle, which offer a wide variety of Italian delicacies *(see p80)*.

7 Sendlinger Straße

This shopping district boasts two main attractions: the late Baroque Asamkirche and, right next door, the Asam-Haus with its impressive façade *(see p68 and pp80–81)*.

Around Marienplatz

9 Pedestrian Zone

Munich's most popular traffic-free shopping zone *(see p68)* starts to the west of Marienplatz and extends right through to Karlsplatz. This is also the location of the late Renaissance Michaelskirche *(see p44)*.

10 National-theater

Next door to the Residenz, the National-theater **(above)** is one of the largest opera stages in the world. This temple-like structure has been destroyed and rebuilt twice in its lifetime *(see p89)*.

8 Residenz

Max-Joseph-Platz is the site of the 130-room Residenz, a palace that was home to the Bavarian monarchs for five centuries. The buildings date back to 1385, when the Neuveste was built in the part of Munich enclosed by city walls. Its monumental façades and courtyards are open to the public, and the Residenz-musueum is housed inside *(see pp16–17)*.

NEED TO KNOW

MAP N3–4 ■ S1–S8: Marienplatz, U3/U6: Marienplatz and Odeonsplatz

Neues Rathaus: (089) 2339 6555. Tours 3:30pm Mon & Fri, 11:30am & 1:30pm Sat. Adm: €10; concessions €8; free for under-18s

Rathaus Tower: 10am–7pm Mon–Fri, to 5pm in winter Adm: €2.50; concessions €1. DA

Glockenspiel: 11am & noon daily; Mar–Oct: also at 5pm

Peterskirche: (089) 2 1023 7760. Tower: 9am–7pm Mon–Fri, 10am–7pm Sat & Sun (until 6pm in winter). Adm: €1.50; concessions €1

Toy Museum (Altes Rathaus): (089) 271 1969. 10am–5:30pm daily. Adm: €4; concessions €1

TOP 10 ★ Frauenkirche

The Frauenkirche – or, more formally, Dom zu Unserer Lieben Frau (Cathedral of Our Dear Lady) – is the largest Gothic hall church in southern Germany. It was built between 1468 and 1488 by Jörg von Halspach and Lucas Rottaler to replace an earlier Romanesque church. The domes atop its two almost 100-m (328-ft) towers, dominate the city's skyline – no buildings are permitted to be built higher.

The Devil's Footprint ①

This footprint (right), complete with spur at the heel, is said to have been made by the devil after losing a bet with the cathedral's builders.

② Bridal Doorway

The southeastern entrance is adorned with delicate figurines and other elaborate embellishments.

④ Choir Carvings

The choir stalls and screens in the chancel display figures and reliefs added between 1495 and 1502 by Erasmus Grasser.

⑤ Vaulted Ceilings

The original star-patterned vaulted ceiling, which was destroyed in World War II, was meticulously restored in 1990–93 (left).

The Emperor's Tomb ③

The intricately carved tomb of Emperor Ludwig IV of Bavaria (right) was completed in 1622 by Hans Krumpper.

6 Organ
The main organ **(above)** is one of four in the cathedral and was built by Georg Jann in 1994. It is a gigantic instrument, with tubes ranging in size from drainpipes to straws.

7 Memminger Altar
From the chancel to the right and left of the Mariensäule (column), it is possible to see parts of the winged Memminger Altar, designed in around 1500 by Claus Strigel.

8 Cathedral Windows
The windows **(left)** were added at various times over the centuries. Some of the original Gothic and stained-glass windows are still in situ.

9 Statue of St Christopher
This figure, carved in around 1525, exemplifies the dramatic style of the late Gothic period.

10 Towers
The two towers complete with Renaissance domes **(above)** were modelled on the Dome of the Rock in Jerusalem.

NEED TO KNOW

MAP M3 ▪ Frauenplatz ▪ S-Bahn and U-Bahn: Marienplatz ▪ (089) 21791 ▪ www.muenchner-dom.de

Open 7:30am–8:30pm daily. No tours during Mass (9am, noon & 5:30pm Mon–Sat, 10am Sun)
Tours: May–Sep: 3pm Tue, Thu & Sun (€6)

Cathedral Shop: 10–11:45am & 12:30–5pm Mon–Sat
South Tower: Currently closed for renovation.

▪ The cathedral hosts organ concerts, choir performances and various other recitals.

▪ In addition to standard tours, there are also themed tours, including one on the history of the cathedral windows.

▪ There are fountains between Frauenplatz and Augustinerstraße, offering respite for tired feet.

▪ **Frauenkirche Guide**
The church has one of Germany's most important bell collections – five from the Middle Ages and two from the Baroque period.

🔟⭐ Residenz

Located in the heart of the city, this former residence of Bavarian kings, home to the Wittelsbach dynasty until 1918, began in 1385 as a moated castle, but grew over the centuries into an extensive complex with ten courtyards. The largest city-centre castle in Germany, it exhibits a mishmash of styles, from the Baroque Cuvilliés-Theater to the Mannerist Reiche Kapelle. Tours are self-guided, so you can take your time exploring the many interiors open to the public.

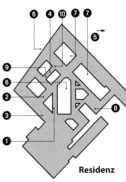

Residenz

1 Antiquarium
Commissioned by Duke Albrecht V, this 69-m (226-ft) long vault **(above)** is embellished with allegorical frescoes, grotesque paintings and Bavarian landscapes.

2 Grüne Galerie
The Reiches Zimmer suite, designed by François Cuvilliés the Elder, is home to the Green Gallery **(left)**, in which Elector Karl Albrecht hosted a great many parties.

3 Schatzkammer
The 16th-century treasury contains the Wittelsbach dynasty's crown jewels, gold reliquaries, porcelain and other treasures.

4 Hofkapelle
This elaborately stuccoed, two-storey chapel was built in 1601–14 by Hans Krumpper. Courtiers would congregate down below, while the ruling family would attend Mass from the upper galleries.

8 Cuvilliés-Theater

This theatre **(left)**, built by François Cuvilliés the Elder in 1751–5, is considered the most beautiful Rococo theatre in Europe. It once staged magnificent Baroque operas and is still used today for performances of all kinds.

5 Hofgarten

Shaded by linden trees on the north side of the Residenz, this Renaissance garden, dating back to 1613, exudes a southern European air. The Temple of Diana, designed by Heinrich Schön the Elder, stands at the heart of the garden's network of pathways.

9 Reiche Kapelle

With its ebony altar, coloured marble and gilded reliefs, Maximilian I's elaborate private chapel (1607) is a prime example of Mannerist architecture.

6 Lions

The front of the Residenz building is guarded by four bronze lions bearing shields. All of their muzzles are worn down, which is due to the local tradition of stroking them for good luck when passing by **(left)**.

10 Staatliche Münz-sammlung

This museum is home to the world's largest collection of coins, alongside banknotes, medals and cut stones, including antique gems.

7 Inner Courtyards

Of the various courtyards, look out for the Grottenhof **(right)** and the octagonal-shaped Brunnenhof. The largest courtyard is the Apothekenhof, while the one by Cuvilliés-Theater is the smallest.

NEED TO KNOW

MAP N3 ■ Residenzstraße 1 ■ U3/U6 & U4/U5: Odeonsplatz ■ (089) 290671 ■ www.residenz-muenchen.de

Residenz: Apr–mid-Oct: 9am–6pm daily; mid-Oct–Mar: 10am–5pm daily. Closed 1 Jan, Shrove Tuesday, 24, 25 & 31 Dec. Wheelchair users may have to be accompanied by a member of staff. Adm: €7; concessions €6. Combined museum/Schatzkammer ticket: €11; concessions €9. Audio guide available

Cuvilliés-Theater: Apr–mid-Oct: 2–6pm Mon–Sat, 9am–6pm Sun & public holidays (Aug–mid-Sep: from 9am daily); mid-Oct–Mar: 2–5pm Mon–Sat, 10am–5pm Sun & public holidays. Adm: €3.50; concessions €2.50

Staatliche Münz-sammlung: Residenzstraße 1 (entrance on Kapellen-hof) ■ (089) 227221 ■ www.staatliche-muenz-sammlung.de

Open 10am–5pm Tue–Sun. Adm: €2.50; concessions €2. All museums: free for under-18s

Some of the Residenz rooms are likely to be closed for renovation.

⭐ Alte Pinakothek

Munich's Pinakotheken, three top-class art galleries, are located in the museum quarter. The Alte Pinakothek was founded by Ludwig I, designed by Leo von Klenze, and opened in 1836. The Neue Pinakothek and Pinakothek der Moderne complete the trio *(see pp20–21)*. The Alte Pinakothek houses collections of Bavarian dukes, electors and kings, as well as the treasures of dissolved monasteries. The museum is undergoing renovation but it remains open to the public. Expect partial closures and relocated exhibits until the end of 2018.

Trojan Horse (Wimmer)

① Brueghel's *Land of Cockaigne*
Pieter Brueghel the Elder, the most significant artist of the Flemish School, offers a satirical depiction of gluttony and idleness (**above**) in this painting from 1567, which is based on a tale by Hans Sachs.

② Botticelli's *Lamentation of Christ*
Sandro Botticelli's painting from around 1490 is renowned for its intense red tones, stark contrasts and curved lines. It is considered one of the great masterpieces of Italian Renaissance painting.

③ Dürer's *Four Apostles*
The gallery's Dürer collection documents his development from *Self-Portrait in Fur Coat* (1500) to the *Four Apostles* (1526), painted two years before his death.

④ Altdorfer's *Battle of Alexander at Issus*
Albrecht Altdorfer's 1529 painting depicts the decisive moment of Alexander the Great's victory over the Persian King Darius (**left**).

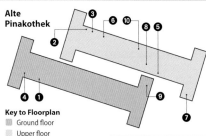

Alte Pinakothek

Key to Floorplan
- Ground floor
- Upper floor

5 Hals' *Willem van Heythuysen*

Frans Hals' painting of the Haarlem cloth merchant is an outstanding example of Dutch portraiture **(above)**.

6 Titian's *Portrait of Charles V*

Titian painted this portrait of the emperor at the imperial court at Augsburg in 1548.

8 Rembrandt's *Descent from the Cross*

Dramatic lighting characterizes the artist's 1633 masterpiece, which was a stark contrast to the idealized representations of Christ typical of the time. The figure in blue is a self-portrait.

9 Holbein's *Presentation of Jesus at the Temple*

This late Gothic piece (1502) by Hans Holbein the Elder forms part of the Kaisheim altar.

10 Rubens' *The Rape of the Daughters of Leucippus*

In this high Baroque masterpiece of 1618 **(above)**, Rubens depicts a mythical tangle of human and horse.

7 El Greco's *Disrobing of Christ*

El Greco created this sombre work in 1580–95. It forms part of an exceptional collection of Spanish paintings **(above)**.

NEED TO KNOW

MAP F3–F4/M2 ▪ Alte Pinakothek: Barer Straße 27, (089) 2380 5216 ▪ Neue Pinakothek: Barer Straße 29, (089) 2380 5195 ▪ Pinakothek der Moderne: Barer Straße 40, (089) 2380 5360 ▪ U2: Theresienstraße, Tram 27, Bus 100 ▪ www.pinakothek.de ▪ DA

Alte Pinakothek:
10am–8pm Tue, 10am–6pm Wed–Sun. Adm: €4; concessions €2; €1 on Sun

Neue Pinakothek:
10am–8pm Wed, 10am–6pm Thu–Mon. Adm: €7; concessions €5; €1 on Sun

Pinakothek der Moderne:
10am–8pm Thu, 10am–6pm Wed & Fri–Sun. Adm: €10; concessions €7; €1 on Sun

▪ There are combined tickets, audio guides and tours available.

▪ The Alte Pinakothek and Pinakothek der Moderne both have cafés, the latter with outdoor seating; the Neue Pinakothek has its own restaurant, also with outdoor seating. All three have museum shops.

Alte Pinakothek Guide
The ground floor is largely given over to German paintings up to around 1500. The upper floor is home to later German works, Dutch Old Masters, the Italian Renaissance, 17th-century French, Flemish and Dutch works, and a Spanish collection.

Neue Pinakothek

Walter Crane's *Neptune's Horses*

1 Crane's *Neptune's Horses*

Walter Crane's 1892 painting **(above)** fuses Pre-Raphaelite expression with Art Nouveau and Symbolist influences.

2 Spitzweg's *The Poor Poet*

Carl Spitzweg's celebrated 1839 painting captures the spirit of the Biedermeier period.

Édouard Manet's *Breakfast in the Studio*

3 Manet's *Breakfast in the Studio*

Édouard Manet's seminal 1868 work of strong light and dark contrasts heralded the beginning of Impressionism, and is one of the highlights of the Neue Pinakothek.

4 Liebermann's *Boys Bathing*

Dating from 1898, this work by Max Liebermann exemplifies the preoccupation of German Impressionists with capturing the play of light in their work.

5 Friedrich's *Ruins at Dusk*

A key theme of Romanticism, ruins symbolize the transience of earthly values. Caspar David Friedrich's 1831 painting is also known as *Church Ruin in the Woods*.

6 Böcklin's *Play of the Waves*

Arnold Böcklin was heavily inspired by classical mythology. This work from 1883 depicts water nymphs, mermaids and sea gods.

7 Canova's *Paris*

Antonio Canova's sculpture of the Trojan prince (1816) is the epitome of pure classicism.

8 Van Gogh's *Sunflowers*

This Munich version (1888) of *Sunflowers* by Vincent van Gogh is a fundamental piece in the collection.

9 Khnopff's *I Lock my Door upon Myself*

This Symbolist work by Belgian artist Fernand Khnopff (1891) is based on a poem by Christina Rossetti.

10 Klimt's *Music*

Gustav Klimt's allegoric representation of Music (1895) in oil and gold bronze is a prime example of the Viennese Secession.

Pinakothek der Moderne

1 The Classic Modern Collection

The Classic Modern encompasses the period from the early 20th century up to 1960 and features works by Kirchner, Nolde, Braque, Picasso, Klee and Beckmann amongst others.

2 Surrealism

The Surrealist pieces in the museum come from the Wormland collection. Among the highlights are Max Ernst's *Fireside Angel* (1937) and Salvador Dali's *The Enigma of Desire* (1929).

3 The Contemporary Art Collection

This section documents the art scene from 1960 onwards and includes works by Bacon, Beuys, Baselitz, Polke, Warhol, de Kooning, Flavin, Wall and Twombly.

4 The Design Museum

Modern utilitarian objects (below) are the theme of this 80,000-strong collection at Die Neue Sammlung – The Design Museum. Exhibits range from Thonet chairs and Pop furniture right through to objects from the world of aerodynamics and digital culture.

5 Installations

Permanent installations include Joseph Beuys' *The End of the Twentieth Century* (1983) and Dan Flavin's *Monument for V. Tatlin* (1964).

6 The Graphic Arts Collection

This collection comprises tens of thousands of drawings and prints, though only a fraction is ever on display at any one time. Highlights include works by Old Masters such as Rembrandt and Michelangelo, in addition to pieces by Cézanne, Baselitz and Wols.

7 Drawings

Among the highlights of this collection are Raphael's red chalk drawing of *Mercury and Psyche* (1517/18) and Franz Marc's *The Tower of Blue Horses* (1912) in ink.

8 The Architecture Collection

Some 350,000 drawings and plans, 100,000 photographs and 500 models are presented in rotating exhibits on the ground floor.

9 Drawings and Sketches

With a firm focus on German architecture from the 18th to the 21st centuries, these exhibits include drawings and sketches by Balthasar Neumann, Leo von Klenze and Le Corbusier.

10 Design Vision

This two-storey display cabinet showcases objects that illuminate the full spectrum of the gallery's collection, ranging from visionary ideas through to everyday objects.

Modern objects displayed in The Design Museum

🔟 ⭐ Englischer Garten

One of the largest inner-city parks in Europe, the Englischer Garten was conceived by Sir Benjamin Thompson (1753–1814), who was awarded the title of Count Rumford by Karl Theodor, Elector of Bavaria. As Bavarian minister of war and a social reformist, Rumford ordered that the marshy banks of the Isar be converted into a park, initially for the use of the army, but it was opened to the people of Munich in 1792. As the park continued to grow, its design was taken over by court gardener Friedrich L von Sckell. Much expanded, it remains the green lung of Munich to this day.

1 Rumford Monument

This monument **(above)** in honour of Count Rumford was erected in 1796 by leading Bavarian sculptor Franz Jakob Schwanthaler.

2 Monopteros

This classical round temple was built in 1836 by Leo von Klenze **(below)**. It sits atop an artificial hill, which is a popular spot all year round, attracting sunbathers in the summer and tobogganists in winter.

3 Kleinhesse-loher See

This lake **(above)** can be found in the northern-most corner of the park. It is the perfect spot to hire a rowing boat or pedalo and mess about on the water. The shores of the lake are home to a scenic beer garden.

4 Surfers on the Eisbach

Undeterred by the icy waters, surfers engage with the Eisbach rapids, at the southernmost tip of the park **(above)**.

6 Chinesischer Turm

The Chinese Tower (left) is one of the city's most emblematic landmarks. Standing five storeys high, the wooden pagoda in the traditional Chinese style dates back to 1789 and has burnt down and been rebuilt several times. At the foot of the tower is one of Munich's best beer gardens.

8 Historisches Karussell

Right next to the Chinesischer Turm is a Biedermeier-style children's roundabout, complete with carriages, sleighs and whimsical wooden animals. It is still in use today.

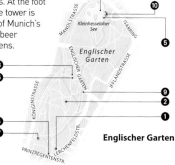

Englischer Garten

5 Friedrich-Ludwig-von-Sckell Monument

This memorial, designed by Klenze in 1824, was built in memory of the park's designer.

7 Japanisches Teehaus

The teahouse and its Japanese garden can be found at the south end of the park on an artificial island in the Schwabinger Bach. Traditional tea ceremonies take place here at weekends in summer, and Japanfest is held around the teahouse each July.

9 Orangerie

The former orangery now serves as an exhibition space.

10 Seehaus

The beer garden belonging to the Seehaus restaurant occupies an idyllic spot on Kleinhesseloher See, partly shaded by the nearby trees. If the weather is good, it stays open out of season.

NEED TO KNOW

MAP GH1–4 U3/U6: Odeonsplatz–Münchner Freiheit; Bus 100: Chinesischer Turm; Tram 18: Tivolistraße

Facts: 376 ha 78 km (49 miles) of pathways (including 12 km/7 miles of bridle paths), 15 km (9 miles) of waterways, and over 100 bridges and jetties 4 restaurants with beer gardens 5 million visitors every year

Chinesischer Turm: Englischer Garten 3; (089) 383 8730. Restaurant open all year round, beer garden May–Sep. Brass band Wed–Sun; folk dancing at the traditional Kocherlball (3rd Sun in July from 6am)

Seehaus: Kleinhesseloher 3; (089) 381 6130. Restaurant and beer garden

Japanisches Teehaus: Königinstraße 4; (089) 224319. Tea ceremony Apr–Oct: Sat & Sun 2, 3, 4 & 5pm

Orangerie: Englischer Garten 1A; only open for exhibitions.

Historisches Karussell: Englischer Garten 4; Apr–Oct: from 2pm daily (from 1pm in the summer holidays)

Following pages Aglaia (1961) by Toni Stadler Jnr in front of the Neue Pinakothek

🔟⭐ Deutsches Museum

The world's largest museum of technology and engineering, founded by Oskar von Miller in 1903, is located in a building on Museumsinsel (museum Island). It is currently undergoing renovation work, due for completion in the next few years. Individual sections will be temporarily closed off, but the museum as a whole remains open. Other branches of the museum include the Verkehrszentrum near the Theresienwiese and the Flugwerft Schleißheim, north of the centre *(see p29)*.

Planet trail sign

4 Planetarium
The planetarium allows visitors to get an unparalleled look at the night skies above Munich and even to step back in history. Thirty-minute shows take place here every day at noon and 2pm.

6 Power Machinery
Steam engines, motors and generators are to be found in this section. Some of these colossal machines, like the Alban high-pressure steam engine from 1839, are veritable works of art.

1 Faraday Cage
The Energy exhibit is home to a high-voltage installation **(above)**, which allows visitors to get close to electrical phenomena. Tours of the Faraday cage are perennially popular (11am, 2 & 4pm daily).

2 Galileo's Workshop
In the Physics section, a reconstruction of Galileo's workshop features a collection of equipment used by the famous Italian astronomer and physicist.

3 Enigma Machine
The Enigma encoding machine built during World War II is a fine example of early information technology.

5 Ewer Maria
Along with countless model ships, the vast exhibition hall of the marine navigation section features several original historical sailboats and steam boats, such as the 1932 steam tugboat *Renzo* and the 1880 wooden fishing vessel *Ewer Maria* **(above)**.

⑨ Mining
Split over three floors, much of the space in the Mining section is built to resemble a real mine *(see p28)*, creating an atmospheric exhibit.

⑩ Musical Instruments
Instruments here range from medieval lutes to the latest synthesizers.

⑦ Pharmaceuticals
The highlight of this fascinating section is a walk-through model of a human cell, the cell wall magnified 350,000 times **(above)**. Visitors can also enjoy a presentation on genetic engineering and the development and production of modern pharmaceuticals.

⑧ Microelectronics
This section is home to some valuable original objects, among them the first telephone, dating from 1863, an AEG radio transmitter from 1913 and a manual switchboard from 1905.

Microelectronics ⑧ — ③ Information technology
Astronomy, observatories, planetarium (levels 4–6) ④
② Physics
⑩ Musical instruments
Ⓙ Marine navigation
Mining ⑨
⑥ Power machinery
Pharmaceuticals ⑦
Key to Floorplan
- Level LG
- Level 0
- Level 1
- Level 2
- Levels 3–6
Mining ⑥
Marine navigation ⑤
① High-voltage installation

NEED TO KNOW

MAP FG5 ▪ Museuminsel 1 ▪ S1–S8: Isartor, Tram 16: Deutsches Museum ▪ (089) 21791 or (089) 217 9333 ▪ www.deutsches-museum.de

Open 9am–5pm daily. Closed 1 Jan, Shrove Tue, Good Fri, 1 May, 1 Nov, 24, 25 & 31 Dec. Adm: €11; concessions €4/€7; combined ticket (for Museumsinsel, Flugwerft and Verkehrszentrum) €16

Planetarium: €2; evening lectures €3. Tours: 2-hour highlights tour at 11am & 2pm; €3. DA

Verkehrszentrum: **MAP J4** ▪ Am Bavariapark 5 ▪ U4/5: Schwanthalerhöhe ▪ (089) 50080 6762

Open 9am–5pm daily. Closed as main museum. Adm: €6; concessions €3.

Overview tours: 11am, 1:30 & 2pm. DA

Flugwerft Schleißheim: Effnerstraße 18, 85764 Oberschleißheim ▪ S1: Oberschleißheim ▪ (089) 315 7140

Open 9am–5pm daily. Closed as main museum. Adm: €6 (€3 concessions). Overview tours: 11am & 3:30pm

Deutsches Museum: Collections

1 Physics and Astronomy

The Physics section features measuring and observation devices, including Foucault's pendulum. Meanwhile, Astronomy has sections on the sun, stars and astrophysics.

2 Pharmaceuticals, Chemistry and Clocks

Examples of traditional craftsmanship are on display in the Clocks exhibit. In Chemistry there's a reconstruction of von Liebig's laboratory, while Pharmaceuticals examines medicinal plants and drug development.

3 Mining, Metals and Agricultural Engineering

The spectacular mine reconstruction in this section **(right)** is complemented by exhibits on the 12,000-year-old history of metallurgy. The agriculture section illustrates the cultivation of cereals and grain, and the brewing process.

4 Tools, Ceramics and Glass

Paper and glass manufacturing, ceramics production from bricks to fine china, and tools from Stone-Age drills to computer-controlled lathes can all be found in this section.

5 Energy and Power Machinery

From original windmills to plasma and fusion technology, this section

Inside the replica mine

features inventions that make our lives easier. The huge steam engines and high-voltage experiments are not to be missed.

6 Marine Navigation

Numerous model ships illustrate several millennia of marine navigation. The rescue cruiser *Theodor Heuss* is displayed in the open-air exhibition space.

7 Historic Aviation

The Origins of Aviation section showcases developments from balloons and airships to the very first engine flights.

8 Water and Civil Engineering

An authentic suspension bridge dominates the exhibition hall, with wall-mounted screens tracking the oscillations as visitors cross over its swaying structure.

9 Kids' Zone

This section is brimming with interactive exhibits designed for young scientists aged three and up.

10 New Technologies

Recent research findings from climate research to nanotechnology and medical technology are presented here.

Lab inside New Technologies

THE BRANCH MUSEUMS

Flugwerft Schleißheim, the Deutsches Museum's branch museum on the history of aviation, is located in an old aeroplane hangar on a historic airfield in Schleißheim *(see p27)*. In addition to the buildings and airfield itself, the site comprises 7,800 square metres (83,958 sq ft) of exhibition space, housing over 50 aeroplanes, helicopters and hang-gliders, plus various instruments and equipment.

At the Verkehrszentrum, or Transport Centre, on Theresienhöhe *(see p27)*, three halls that were once home to the Messe München trade fair now house historic locomotives, cars, carriages and bicycles. This part of the Deutsches Museum represents the largest transport museum in the world, offering a comprehensive exploration of urban transport and travel as a whole.

FLUGWERFT AND VERKEHRSZENTRUM HIGHLIGHTS

1 Fokker D VII fighter aircraft (World War I)

2 Douglas DC-3 commercial aircraft, 1943

3 Heinkel He 111, bomber aircraft (World War II)

4 Lockheed F-104 Starfighter

5 Dornier Do 31, vertical lift-off aircraft

6 *Puffing Billy* (first locomotive in the world)

7 Drais wheel

8 Benz motor car (the first automobile in the world)

9 Rumpler "Tropfenwagen" (aerodynamic car, 1921)

10 NSU Delphin III (motorcycle, 1956)

Street scene at the Verkehrszentrum

Inside Flugwerft Schleißheim

📻 ⭐ Schloss Nymphenburg

To celebrate the birth of their son Max Emanuel in 1662, the Elector Ferdinand Maria and his wife Henriette Adelaide of Savoy commissioned Agostino Barelli to build a summer palace to the west of Munich. Building began in 1664, and the wings and annexe buildings were added from 1701 onwards. Over the course of 300 years, the original ornamental garden was expanded into a vast park comprising Baroque gardens, a system of canals, and small pavilions dotted throughout the grounds.

The Palace 1

Elector Max Emanuel and Karl Albrecht expanded the original villa by adding buildings designed by Enrico Zuccalli and Joseph Effner. Arcaded galleries connect them to the main building **(right)**.

2 Gallery of Beauties

Ludwig I commissioned court artist Joseph Stieler to create these portraits of noblewomen, townswomen and dancers, including the ravishing Lola Montez **(above)**, Irish mistress of King Ludwig I.

3 Steinerner Saal

The Rococo embellishment in the ballroom was created by Johann B Zimmermann and Cuvilliés the Elder in the reign of Max III Joseph.

4 Lackkabinett

This room was designed in 1764 by Cuvilliés the Elder. Chinese black laquer motifs on wood panelling are reprised in the Rococo ceiling fresco.

6 Marstall-museum

This building houses carriages and sleighs that once belonged to the Bavarian rulers, including the gilded state coach of Ludwig II.

5 Monopteros

Between 1804 and 1823, Friedrich L von Sckell created a landscaped park behind the palace. It was during this time that the Monopteros (Apollo temple) was built on the Badenburger See **(above).**

7 Palace Gardens

Symmetrically designed French gardens to the rear of the palace give way to an English-style landscaped park, which was created by using the existing forest. The gardens are home to a number of individual pavilions.

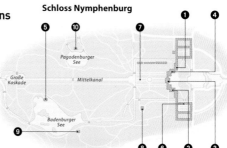

Schloss Nymphenburg

9 Badenburg

Featuring a ballroom and two-storey bathing hall complete with heated pool, this pavilion is definitely worth a visit. Three of the rooms are lined with Chinese-style wallpaper.

10 Pagodenburg

This 18th-century pavilion with an octagonal floor plan combines Western and Eastern ornamentation to stunning effect.

Amalienburg 8

Built by Cuvilliés the Elder between 1734 and 1739 for the Electress Amalia, this small hunting lodge (right) is a masterpiece of European Rococo.

NEED TO KNOW

MAP AB2–3 ■ Tram 17: Schloss Nymphenburg ■ (089) 179080 ■ www.schloss-nymphenburg.de ■ DA

Children and under-18s free.

Palace and Marstall-museum:
Apr–mid-Oct: 9–6pm daily; mid-Oct–Mar: 10am–4pm daily. Closed 1 Jan, Shrove Tuesday, 24, 25 & 31 Dec.

Adm: Palace €6; concessions €5. Museums €4.50; concessions €3.50. Combined ticket (including pavilions) €11.50; concessions €9; in winter €8.50, concessions €6.50

No regular tours (various themed tours available, see website); audio guides available

Park: Jan–Mar, Nov & Dec: 6am–6pm daily; May–Sep: 6am–9:30pm daily; Apr & Oct: 6am–8pm daily

Pavilions: Apr–mid-Oct: 9am–6pm daily. Adm: €4.50; concessions €3.50

Museum Mensch und Natur: Occupies one of the wings of Schloss Nymphenburg (see p127).

■ The Schlosscafé im Palmenhaus is the perfect place to take a break from sightseeing; open 11am–6pm daily; (089) 175309.

🔟 ⭐ Olympiapark

In preparation for the 1972 Olympic Games, a former airfield and parade ground were transformed into an Olympic park, featuring hills, an artificial lake, a communications tower and sports facilities across an area measuring 3 sq km (1 sq mile). Designed by architectural firm Behnisch & Partners, the elegant, airy Olympic complex, complete with transparent, curved, tensile roof, is still considered to be a masterpiece of modern architecture.

1 BMW Welt
BMW's car delivery and exhibition centre **(below)** is the epitome of dynamism and elegance. It contains restaurants and shops and hosts events *(see p129)*.

4 Olympic Skating Rink
The skating rink is the perfect place to bring the kids on winter days. In the evening there's disco skating. Ice skates are available for hire.

2 Father Timofej's Chapel
This Russian Orthodox chapel was built on this site (without a permit) in 1951 by Russian exiles Timofej and Natascha.

5 Kino am Olympiasee
Enjoy a relaxed summer evening at the open-air cinema by the lake, with films often shown in their original language **(below)**.

6 Olympiaturm
A high-speed lift transports visitors to the observation deck and revolving restaurant at the top of this 290 m (951 ft) tower **(above)**. The views across the site and city are incredible – when the Föhn winds are blowing, you can even see the Alps. The restaurant takes 49 minutes to complete a full revolution.

3 Olympic Hall
This venue holds up to 15,500 spectators beneath a large section of the tensile roof, which is suspended from 58 pylons. In addition to sporting events, the hall also hosts concerts and trade fairs.

Sea Life 8

This aquarium is home to an array of underwater creatures, including seahorses, rays and tropical fish **(right)**. The shark tunnel is a highlight *(see p51)*.

9 Lake and Park

Much of the site is purpose-built, including the lake – boats can be hired in summer – and the hills, created by covering piles of war debris with turf.

10 Olympia-stadion

With a capacity of 69,250 spectators, the Olympic stadium is now used to host concerts and events.

Olympiapark

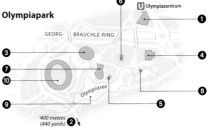

GEORG- | BRAUCHLE-RING

Olympiasee

400 metres
(440 yards)

U Olympiazentrum

Olympia Schwimmhalle 7

One of the largest in Europe, this aquatic centre **(right)** has five pools, a 10 m (33 ft) diving board, saunas, sun-bathing areas, a gym and wellness features.

NEED TO KNOW

MAP DE1–2
- Spiridon-Louis-Ring 21
- U3: Olympiazentrum
- (089) 30670 ■ www.olympiapark.de

Olympiastadion:
Open daily; closed 24 & 31 Dec. Adm: €3.50, concessions €2.50; family ticket (4 people) €8.50. Stadium tour: €8; concessions €6

Olympiaturm: 9am–midnight Mon–Sat. Adm: €7; concessions €5; family ticket (4 people) €18; free for under-6s

Olympia Schwimmhalle: Closed for renovation until summer 2018; some areas remain open. www.swm.de

....

■ The Olympiastadion runs tours and activities based around its tensile roof, including abseiling. Prices range from €43 to €73. Call (089) 30 672414.

■ The on-site railway takes visitors on a journey through the history of the Olympic park. Call (089) 30 672414 or 30 672415.

■ The Theatron amphitheatre is the venue for free open-air summer concerts in August *(see p75)*.

🔟 ⭐ Oktoberfest

With around 6.5 million visitors consuming 7 million litres (12 million pints) of beer, 500,000 roast chickens and 100 oxen, Munich's Oktoberfest is the largest beer festival in the world. At the foot of the Bavaria statue, the Theresienwiese is transformed with beer tents run by traditional breweries, fairground rides and vendors selling gingerbread hearts, roast chicken and fresh pretzels. Whether they opt for traditional costume or not, visitors and locals alike love to indulge in this biggest of Bavarian bashes.

1 O'Zapft Is!
At noon on the first Saturday of Oktoberfest, the mayor of Munich taps the first beer barrel in the Schottenhamel tent and declares to the crowds "O'zapft is!" as the beer starts to flow.

2 Bavaria Statue
In 1843, Ludwig I commissioned Leo von Klenze to build the Rohmeshalle (Hall of Fame) on the Theresien-höhe, which houses the busts of famous Bavarians. The colossal statue embodying Bavaria rises up in front. A platform inside its head offers a spectacular view of the Wiesn area.

5 Hearts
Every year, old and new messages appear on these traditional gingerbread hearts on sale at the Wiesn. They make perfect souvenirs **(left)**, along with the 1-litre Maß beer glass.

3 Memorial
On 26 September 1980, a bomb exploded at the Wiesn, killing 13 people and injuring over 200 more. A stele stands here as a reminder of this neo-Nazi attack.

4 Weißbier Carousel
One of the quirkier of the Oktoberfest drinking spots, this is the largest mobile bar on a carousel in the world – for adults only **(right)**.

9 Arrival of the Wiesn-Wirte

The arrival of the landlords (on the Saturday) is the prelude to the opening of the Wiesn. Their carriages are drawn by brightly decorated show horses from the brewery (left).

8 Beer Tents

In the large beer tents like the Pschorr-Bräurosl (left), alcohol is king. Patrons link arms and sway to the music of brass bands, and challenge each other to drink another Maß of beer.

10 Rides

With traditional fairground attractions such as the merry-go-round and Ferris wheel, and thrill rides, such as Skyfall and Olympia (below), there's something for everyone, from kids through to adrenaline junkies.

6 Beim Schichtl

Welcome to the cabaret – this theatre has been a Wiesn fixture since 1871. You can still watch traditional acts today, such as the "beheading" of an audience member at the guillotine.

7 Flea Circus

Another old-time Oktoberfest tradition not to be missed, these tiny trained creatures and their masters have been entertaining spectators on the Wiesn every year since 1948.

NEED TO KNOW

MAP JK4–5 ■ U4/5: Theresienwiese, U3/6: Goetheplatz or Poccistraße ■ mid-Sep–early Oct ■ www.oktoberfest.de

Beer Tents: 10am–11:30pm Mon–Fri (from 9am Sat & Sun); Käfer's Wiesenschänke until 1am

Rides: 10am–11:30pm Mon–Thu (until midnight Fri and Sat)

Kiosks: 10am–11:30pm Mon–Thu (until midnight Fri and Sat)

Family days: Lower prices every Tue noon–6pm

■ Oktoberfest has its own service centre complete with police station, health centre, lost property and lost child point, as well as luggage storage, an ATM and even a post office.

■ The Oide Wiesn, a nostalgic Old Oktoberfest in period costume, with traditional marquees and stalls, is held every two years at the southern end of the Theresienwiese.

TOP 10 ⭐ Neuschwanstein

An idealized vision of a knight's castle on the outside and a homage to Wagner's operas on the inside, Neuschwanstein was Ludwig II's most ambitious project. During the same period, he also commissioned two French-style castles: Linderhof and Herrenchiemsee. Around 1.5 million visitors each year visit Neuschwanstein, and it is consequently busy all year round. But don't let this put you off – a day trip from Munich out to Füssen in the Schwangau is unmissable.

Throne Hall 1

Gold, saints and a touch of Byzantium: the throne hall **(right)** is modelled in part after Munich's Allerheiligen-Hofkirche and the Hagia Sophia in Istanbul. This ceremonial hall extends over the third and fourth floors – the throne was originally supposed to stand like an altar in the apse.

2 Bedroom

In contrast to the romanticism of the rest of the living quarters, the bedroom is in a Gothic style complete with elaborately carved oak panelling. Scenes from Wagner's *Tristan and Isolde* decorate the walls.

3 Grotto

Moving between the living room and study, visitors pass through a small grotto **(left)**, where a waterfall flowed during the king's lifetime. The larger Venus grotto, complete with an artificial lake, is located in the park of Linderhof Palace *(see p134).*

4 Dining Room

Dishes were transported in a lift from the kitchen three storeys below to the dining room, where the reclusive king took most of his meals, usually on his own. The murals in this predominantly red room depict the tradition of the minstrel's song.

9 The Building
The foundation stone was laid in 1869, the gatehouse completed in 1873, and the palace finished in 1884 **(left)**. Work continued, with the king constantly altering plans, until his death. The keep and knight's bath were never finished.

5 Winter Garden
Adjoining the grotto, the winter garden affords a spectacular view of the Allgäu region through its large windows.

6 Hohen-schwangau
Ludwig spent part of his childhood and youth in this summer palace **(below)**, which is set in wildly romantic scenery.

7 Minstrel's Room
The castle's largest room was influenced by the ceremonial hall of the Wartburg in Eisenach. Walls are adorned with the Legend of Percival **(below)**.

8 Chapel
The chapel's altar and murals depict Louis IX, the beatified monarch of France and namesake of Ludwig II, king of Bavaria.

10 Study
Ludwig's study is filled with pictures from Wagner's opera *Tannhäuser*. On his desk is a fanciful writing set in the shape of *Lohengrin*.

NEED TO KNOW

Schwangau bei Füssen
■ (083) 62 930830 ■ www.neuschwanstein.de

Ticket Centre: Apr–mid-Oct: 8am–5pm daily; mid-Oct–Mar: 9am–3pm daily

Castle: Apr–mid-Oct: 9am–6pm daily; mid-Oct–Mar: 10am–4pm daily; closed 1 Jan, Shrove Tuesday, 24, 25 & 31 Dec

Adm: €13; concessions €12; including Hohen-schwangau: €24, concessions €21; free for under-18s

■ Tickets (with an exact start time) are only available from the Hohenschwangau ticket centre, located below the palace. Expect to queue for tickets in peak season.

■ Thirty-minute guided tours are the only way to visit the palace. Tours are available for wheelchair users if booked in advance. Family tours are available in the school holidays, at weekends and on public holidays.

■ The walk from the ticket centre to the castle takes 30–40 minutes; horse-drawn carriages and a shuttle bus are available.

■ The former Grandhotel Alpenrose in Hohen-schwangau is now home to the Museum der bayerischen Könige (Museum of Bavarian Kings); Alpseestraße 28, (083) 62926 4640.

The Top 10 of Everything

The façade of Museum Brandhorst:
36,000 ceramic rods in 23 colours

🔟 Moments in Munich's History

1 1158: Foundation of the City

Henry the Lion, Duke of Bavaria, tore down the old salt bridge in 1157–8 and erected a new crossing over the Isar river just a few kilometres further south. There, the small market town of Munichen developed into the royal city of Munich. The day on which the Hohenstaufen Emperor Friedrich Barbarossa awarded the town the right to hold a market and mint coins (14 June 1158) is still celebrated as Munich's birthday.

Ludwig the Bavarian (1967) by Hans Wimmer

Henry the Lion, Duke of Bavaria

2 1240–1918: The Wittelsbach Dynasty

The Wittelsbachs are one of the oldest noble families in Germany. Following the deposition of Henry the Lion, the Duchy of Bavaria was passed on to Otto I in 1180. From 1240 onwards, the Wittelsbach dynasty was instrumental in defining the evolution of the city. They graduated from simple dukes to electors and finally to kings. Ludwig I commissioned classical public buildings in Munich, whereas Ludwig II built enormous, fairy-tale palaces. The last member of the Wittelsbach dynasty, Ludwig III, fled Bavaria after World War I.

3 1328: Ludwig the Bavarian – Holy Roman Emperor

In 1314, Duke Ludwig IV ("the Bavarian") was elected king of Germany. In 1328, he was crowned emperor of the Holy Roman Empire.

4 1442: Expulsion of the Jews from Munich

Following pogroms against the Jews in the 13th and 14th centuries, Duke Albrecht III gave the order to expel all Jews from Upper Bavaria in 1442.

5 1806: Capital of the Kingdom of Bavaria

In the wake of the Napoleonic redrafting of Europe, the electorate of Bavaria was elevated to a kingdom, with Munich its capital and royal residence. The boundaries of Bavaria at that time were roughly the same as they are today.

6 1848: March Revolution – Abdication of Ludwig I

In 1848, revolutionary uprisings reached Munich, culminating in the storming of the Zeughaus (armoury, now the Stadtmuseum). Having lost the confidence of the court and the bourgeoisie (in part because of an affair with the dancer Lola Montez), Ludwig I was forced to abdicate.

7 1918–19: November Revolution and Räterepublik

On 8 November 1918, socialist Kurt Eisner proclaimed the "Free State of Bavaria" in the Mathäserbräu building and became president for a brief period. Following his assassination on 21 February 1919, *Räterepubliken*

(Soviet republics) emerged in Munich and other Bavarian cities, although these were quickly suppressed by the government.

After the Assassination, **Bachrach-Bareé**

8 1935–45: "Capital of the Movement"

Hitler's party, the NSDAP, grew out of a small nucleus that began in Munich. As early as 1923, Hitler attempted his first coup ("Hitlerputsch") against the Weimar Republic. Munich was given the title "Capital of the Movement" in 1935, after the Nazis seized power.

9 1962: Schwabing Riots

In the summer of 1962, harmless buskers were a catalyst for violent clashes between youths and the Munich police forces that lasted for several days. These events inspired the city to rethink its hard-line policy on police intervention.

10 1972: Olympic Games

Munich hosted the Olympic Games in 1972. The event was overshadowed by a terrorist attack against the Olympic team from Israel.

Munich's Olympic Stadium

FAMOUS CITIZENS

1 Asam brothers
Cosmas Damian (1687–1739) and Egid Quirin (1692–1750) Asam were the chief proponents of the Bavarian Rococo movement.

Egid Quirin Asam

2 Maximilian Joseph von Montgelas
The aristocratic Montgelas (1759–1838) is the politician widely acknowledged as the creator of the modern Bavarian state.

3 Ludwig I
Numerous magnificent buildings were built by King Ludwig I (1786–1868). In 1826, he transferred the university from Landshut to Munich.

4 Lola Montez
As the mistress of Ludwig I, Lola Montez (1818–61) is said to have had great influence on the sovereign.

5 Ludwig II
"Kini" Ludwig II (1845–86) has gone down in history as the "fairy-tale king". His death in the Starnberger See remains a mystery to this day.

6 Franz von Lenbach
The "Painter Prince" (1836–1904) was renowned for his portraits and had a huge influence on Munich's art scene.

7 Franz von Stuck
Stuck (1863–1928) was a co-founder of the Munich Secession. His Art Nouveau villa is now a museum *(see p111)*.

8 Thomas Mann
Nobel Laureate in Literature, Mann (1875–1955) spent some of his younger life in Munich.

9 Karl Valentin
Cabaret artist, clown and comedian Karl Valentin (1882–1948), often dubbed the German Charlie Chaplin, has a museum dedicated to him *(see p82)*.

10 Scholl Siblings
Hans (1918–43) and Sophie (1921–43) Scholl were active in the "White Rose" resistance group in the early years of World War II. They were denounced in 1943 and executed.

TOP 10 Museums and Galleries

Pinakothek der Moderne, designed by architect Stephan Braunfels

1 Pinakotheken

Known collectively as the Pinakotheken, the Alte and Neue Pinakothek and the Pinakothek der Moderne house the city's major art collections *(see pp18–21)*.

2 Deutsches Museum

There's tech fun for young and old at this unsurpassed science and engineering museum *(see pp26–9)*.

3 Bayerisches Nationalmuseum

With its variety of cultural and historical collections, the national museum is one of the largest of its kind in Europe. Its exhibits range from Gothic sculptures and precious wall hangings through to clocks. The folklore section has a collection of cribs *(see p105)*.

Byzantine art, Bayerisches Nationalmuseum

4 Münchner Stadtmuseum

This museum *(see p80)* occupies Munich's former armoury and stables, along with various other buildings. Documenting the history and culture of the city, its permanent exhibits include sections on puppetry/showmanship, photography and National Socialism in Munich. It is also home to the Film Museum where many silent films have been pieced back together *(see p54)*.

5 Glyptothek and Staatliche Antikensammlungen

The Glyptothek's exquisite collection of Greek and Roman sculptures and bas-reliefs includes 2,500-year-old gable sculptures from the temple of Aphaea, whose original colouring has been restored. Antique jewellery, bronzes and Greek ceramics are on display in the Antikensammlungen *(see p97)*.

6 Städtische Galerie im Lenbachhaus

Lenbachhaus – once the villa and studio of master painter Franz von Lenbach – contains the famous collection of works from the Blue Rider group *(see p97)*. The expanded, renovated complex also holds a large collection of 19th-century German art, while its 20th-century works include artist's rooms, photography, and installations and sculptures by Joseph Beuys.

(7) Jüdisches Museum München

This museum reflects the breadth of Jewish history, art and culture in Munich, and hosts a series of special exhibits *(see p80)*.

(8) Museum Villa Stuck

Preserved in its original Art Nouveau style, the villa of Secessionist Franz von Stuck (1863–1928) houses a permanent exhibition in the living rooms, with paintings by the master himself, as well as special exhibitions in the adjoining studio *(see p111)*.

(9) Haus der Kunst

Today, Adolf Hitler's grandiose, monumental building (1932–7) is used as a venue for international art exhibitions *(see p104)*.

(10) Museum Brandhorst

This museum catches the eye before you step through the doors thanks to its dazzling façade of colourful ceramic rods. The building is home to an impressive collection of modern and contemporary art including pieces Cy Twombly, Andy Warhol, Joseph Beuys and Damien Hirst, to name but a few *(see p98)*.

The colourful façade of Museum Brandhorst

OTHER MUSEUMS AND GALLERIES

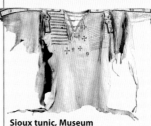

Sioux tunic, Museum Fünf Kontinente

1 Archäologische Staatssammlung
This museum presents prehistoric, Roman and medieval exhibits *(see p106)*.

2 Staatliches Museum Ägyptischer Kunst
Art from Egypt is the main attraction at this museum *(see p98)*.

3 Deutsches Theatermuseum
Located in the Hofgarten arcades, this museum covers the history of German theatre *(see p92)*.

4 Paläontologisches Museum
Archaeopteryx bavarica, a prehistoric bird, is a highlight at this dinosaur museum *(see p100)*.

5 Valentin Karlstadt Musäum
Curios relating to Karl Valentin and his sidekick, Liesl Karlstadt, can be found in the tower of the Isartor *(see p82)*.

6 Sammlung Schack
This collection showcases 19th-century masterpieces from the German art world, including works by Von Böcklin, Spitzweg and Schwind *(see p105)*.

7 Alpines Museum
A museum dedicated to the mountains, with a garden exhibit *(see p112)*.

8 Museum Fünf Kontinente
This museum has hosted global cultural exhibits since 1926 – from the oldest kayak in North America to a replica Shiva temple *(see p112)*.

9 Kunsthalle der Hypo-Kulturstiftung
Outstanding contemporary art exhibitions *(see p91)*.

10 Lothringer 13
MAP Q5 ▪ Lothringer Straße 13
Modern multimedia is on display in this converted factory.

ⓉⓄⓅ10 **Places of Worship**

Choir figures by Erasmus Grasser, Frauenkirche

1 Frauenkirche

Munich's 15th-century cathedral dominates the city's skyline with its twin towers *(see pp14–15)*.

2 Asamkirche

Officially known as the Church of St John of Nepomuk, this late Baroque structure, which was designed, financed and built in the 18th century by the Asam brothers, features opulent ceiling frescoes depicting the eponymous saint. It nestles between two houses, one of which belonged to the Asams *(see p81)*.

3 Ludwigskirche

Friedrich von Gärtner built this church (1829–43), which is flanked by two towers in Italian Romanesque style. Inside, the *Judgment Day* fresco by Peter von Cornelius is the second-largest church fresco in the world and definitely worth a visit *(see p103)*.

4 Michaelskirche

MAP M3 ▪ Neuhauser Straße 6 ▪ 7am–9pm daily ▪ www.st-michael-muenchen.de

St Michael's Church today lies right in the heart of the pedestrian zone. Built for the Jesuits and completed in 1597, it is the largest late Renaissance church north of the Alps, with the second-largest barrel vault in the world after St Peter's in Rome.

Its crypt contains the sarcophagi of Elector Maximilian I and Ludwig II. Look out for the bronze figure of St Michael battling the dragon, dating from 1585, on the east façade.

5 Peterskirche

The oldest parish church in the city (dating from the 13th century) is affectionately known as "Alter Peter" (Old Pete). Its interior is an eclectic mix of Gothic, Baroque and Rococo styles. Brave the 302 steps to the top of the Renaissance tower for superlative views over the old town *(see pp78–9)*.

The ornate ceiling of Peterskirche

6 Theatinerkirche

The Theatinerkirche on Odeonsplatz stands out from the crowd with its bright yellow façade and pure white interior. Construction of this church, which is also called St Cajetan, began in 1663 to mark the birth of the heir to Elector Ferdinand. It is the most Italianate of all the churches in Munich (see p91).

**Façade detail,
Klosterkirche St Anna**

7 Klosterkirche and Pfarrkirche St Anna

MAP P3 ▪ St-Anna-Straße 19/Sankt-Anna-Platz 5 ▪ Open 6am–7pm/ 8am–6pm daily ▪ www.erzbistum-muenchen.de/StAnnaMuenchen

The Lehel district is home to Munich's earliest Rococo church, built by Johann Michael Fischer in 1727–33. The church's interior design can be attributed mainly to the Asam brothers. Construction of the nearby Neo-Romanesque parish church of St Anna took place much later, in 1887–92.

8 Synagoge Ohel Jakob

Munich's main synagogue, Ohel Jakob ("Jacob's tent") in Sankt-Jakobs-Platz, forms part of the city's Jewish centre, together with its Jewish Museum and the Israelite Community of Munich. Dating from 2006, this cube-shaped building is crowned with a glass structure and bronze metallic grid that allows light to flood in. Its sturdy construction, with its irregular, unpolished stonework, is reminiscent of the Western Wall in Jerusalem. Visits are by prearranged tour only (see p80).

9 Damenstiftskirche St Anna

MAP M3–4 ▪ Damenstiftstraße 1 ▪ Open 8am–8pm daily

Originally a convent for the Sisters of the Salesian Order in the Hacken quarter of Munich's old town, St Anna's church is now a school. The late Baroque building dates from 1735, and both the façade and the interior were designed by the Asam brothers. After the church's destruction in World War II, its frescoes were recreated in sepia.

10 Heiliggeistkirche

MAP N4 ▪ Tal 77 ▪ Open 7am–noon & 3–6pm daily ▪ www.heilig-geist-muenchen.de

This church on Viktualienmarkt is one of the oldest in Munich. The 13th century saw the construction of a hospital church on this site, followed in 1392 by a Gothic basilica. In 1724, it was remodelled in Baroque style. The interior blends Gothic and late Baroque. The stucco work is by the Asam brothers.

TOP 10 **Parks and Gardens**

The manicured grounds of the Alter Botanischer Garten

1 Botanischer Garten
Created in Schlosspark Nymphenburg in 1914, this is one of the most important botanical gardens in the world. Some 14,000 plant species from around the globe are cultivated here *(see p129)*.

2 Englischer Garten
For Munich's residents, the Englischer Garten is a recreational paradise in the heart of the city. Every summer, thousands flock to lounge on its lawns, ride their bikes and jog or skate around the many pathways, while the Kleinhesseloher

Enjoying the sun, Englischer Garten

lake brims with boats. For a spot of welcome refreshment, enjoy a cold brew in one of the park's four beer gardens *(see pp22–3)*.

3 Schlosspark Nymphenburg
Enclosed by a wall, this 2-km (1-mile) wide park stretches west from the Nymphenburg palace. Picturesque pavilions and follies are scattered throughout the park, which has been declared a nature reserve to protect its 300-year-old trees *(see pp30–31)*.

4 Westpark
Westpark was created in 1983 for the International Horticultural Exposition. An area of 72 ha (178 acres) was landscaped with numerous artificial hills, pathways, a lake and ponds. The lakeside stage hosts concerts and plays and screens films in summer *(see p121)*.

5 Alter Botanischer Garten
MAP L3 ▪ **Sophienstraße 7**
The former Botanischer Garten was once located in this small park, which was also home to the 1854 Glaspalast before it burned down in 1931. Conveniently located near the pedestrian zone between Stachus

and the Hauptbahnhof, it now serves as the perfect oasis for relaxing after a shopping spree.

6 Bavariapark

This small park, which lies directly behind the statue of *Bavaria*, was established between 1826 and 1831. Today, it is a great spot to take a break from the hustle and bustle of Oktoberfest (see p119).

7 Hofgarten

The Hofgarten on the north side of the Residenz was created in the style of Italian Renaissance gardens. Bounded on two sides by long arcades, it has rows of linden, chestnut and maple trees that provide welcome shade for boules players in the summer. On balmy summer evenings, tango aficionados meet up for dancing at the Temple of Diana, a twelve-sided pavilion which is topped with a shallow dome, and located in the centre of the park.

8 Luitpoldpark

Created in celebration of Prince Regent Luitpold's 90th birthday in 1911, this park was extended in 1950 to include a hill built out of rubble, the Luitpoldhügel. From here there's a fine view of the city – on clear days, you can see all the way to the Alps (see p106).

9 Hirschgarten

This garden's wild deer enclosure serves as a reminder of its former function as a hunting park for the nobility. The park is now popular amongst lovers of recreational sports and its beer garden is said to be the largest in the world (see p128).

10 Isarauen and Rosengarten

MAP E6 ▪ Open summer: 8am–8pm daily; winter: 9am–4pm daily

A long stretch of the Isarauen river meadows forms another of Munich's welcome green spaces. South of the Wittelsbach Brücke is the rose garden – an oasis of tranquillity in the busy city. The small complex also includes an aromatic garden, a garden with poisonous plants and a touch garden for the visually impaired.

The Temple of Diana in the Hofgarten

🔟 Off the Beaten Track

Stargazing at the Bayerische Volkssternwarte München

① Bayerische Volks-sternwarte München

MAP H6 ▪ Rosenheimer Straße 45h ▪ Tours Apr–Aug: 9pm Mon–Fri, Sep–Mar: 8pm Mon–Fri ▪ Adm ▪ www.sternwarte-muenchen.de

This public observatory was established by a group of amateur astronomers after World War II. In addition to the telescopes on the observation platform, it also has a planetarium and hosts exhibitions and lectures by astronomers. There are also tours aimed at children.

② Designer U-Bahn Stations

Munich's U-Bahn stations really pack a punch: the Marienplatz mezzanine is painted a rich orange-red; lighting designer Ingo Maurer had some great fun with blue at Münchner Freiheit; and Westfriedhof is awash with red, yellow and blue. Georg-Brauchle-Ring features a whole host of different colours, while Candidplatz is embellished with rainbow effects. In 2014, Munich's U-Bahn trains won the German Design Award.

③ Der Verrückte Eismacher

MAP N1 ▪ Amalienstraße 77 ▪ Open daily

With ice cream flavours ranging from the fairly traditional, such as nutty–chocolate, melon or kiwi lime, to the more unusual – cheese-and-chive, beer or asparagus, for example – this popular parlour offers a long list of extraordinary concoctions that changes on a daily basis.

④ Summer Tango

MAP N2 & P4 ▪ Hofgarten and Praterinsel

The unofficial meeting point of Munich's tango fans is the Temple of Diana in the Hofgarten *(see p17)*. The otherwise strict site management allows dancers to take part in salsa (Wed and Sun), swing dance (Sun afternoon) and tango (Fri) sessions. Another of these meeting points can be found in the inner courtyard of the former distillery on the Praterinsel.

Rainbow shades at Candidplatz U-Bahn station

5 Löwenturm am Rindermarkt

MAP N4 ■ Rindermarkt 9

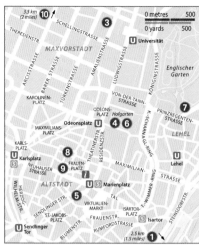

The origins of this 12th-century, 23-m (75-ft) high tower are a bit of a mystery. It was presumably part of the town ramparts, but could also have been a water tower. Unfortunately, it isn't possible to access the interior to see its ribbed vaults and frescos.

6 Hofgarten Boules

MAP N2 ■ Hofgarten (north side)

The Hofgarten has been a popular meeting point for boules players for over 40 years. When the weather is good, they flock to the park to play, lending it a Mediterranean atmosphere. There's a boules tournament here every July, but you can watch players enjoying a game throughout the summer months.

Boules players in front of the arcades of the Hofgarten

7 Fräulein Grüneis

MAP P2 ■ Lerchenfeldstraße 1a ■ Open daily until dusk

On the banks of the Eisbach in the Englischer Garten, not far from where the surfers hang out, there was once a little toilet block. It was then transformed into a pleasant café kiosk serving exclusively organic goodies, including coffee, sandwiches and cakes. Hot lunch dishes are served daily.

8 Michael Jackson Memorial

MAP M3 ■ Promenadeplatz

The statue of the composer Orlande de Lassus in Promenadeplatz is adorned with countless flowers, candles and pictures of the King of Pop. Michael Jackson fans flock here to remember their idol, who used to stay at the nearby Bayerischer Hof.

9 Bronze Model of the City

MAP M3 ■ Frauenplatz

The Frauenkirche serves as the backdrop for this bronze model of Munich's old town, created by Egbert Broerken in 2005. Not only does it help those with visual impairments to find their bearings, but it provides a wonderfully tactile and visual experience for all.

10 Olympia-Alm

MAP E1 ■ Martin-Luther-King-Weg 8 ■ Open noon–midnight daily

The highest beer garden in Munich perches on top of the Olympiaberg at 564 m (1,850 ft). Originally just a kiosk to serve the workers constructing the Olympic Park in 1972, it now offers beer and a selection of hearty Bavarian fare, including Glühwein in winter.

🔟 Munich for Children

1 Olympiapark
Kids who enjoy sport will love the range of activities on offer at the Olympic Park. Whether it's the aquatic centre, beach volleyball court, ski slope, boat centre, streetball court or – for older kids – climbing tours on the tent roof, the jam-packed programme at Olympiapark is the best in the city *(see pp32–3)*.

2 Tierpark Hellabrunn
Highlights of the city zoo include an elephant show, polar bear talk, and sea lion training, as well as the regular feeding times. For younger kids, there's also a petting zoo, play areas and "Kinderland". Be sure to experience one of the animal walks, where you can get up close to the llamas or ponies *(see pp120–21)*.

3 Kindermuseum München
MAP L3 ▪ Arnulfstraße 3 ▪ (089) 5404 6440 ▪ Open 2–5pm Tue–Fri, 10am–5pm Sat, Sun and public/school holidays ▪ Adm ▪ www.kindermuseum-muenchen.de
This children's museum offers interactive exhibits, workshops and plenty of games to keep the little ones occupied.

Hands-on exhibit, Deutsches Museum

Blowing bubbles, Kindermuseum

4 Deutsches Museum
Older children will be fascinated by many of the displays at this museum. There's also a kids' zone for the younger ones (ages 3 and up). The interactive exhibits allow children to experience physics first hand. They're sure to enjoy both the Technisches Spielzeug (Technical Toys) section and the planet walk from the sun to Pluto, which takes around an hour *(see pp26–9)*.

5 Marionettentheater
MAP M4 ▪ Blumenstraße 32 ▪ (089) 265712 ▪ Adm ▪ www.muema-theater.de
Munich's oldest puppet theatre, founded in 1858, is housed in a small gabled and colonnaded temple dating back to 1900. Performances are enthusiastically received by young and old alike, and shows here can include anything from children's mysteries to *The Magic Flute*.

6 Bavaria Filmstadt
Film and television productions are still made at these studios, which offer a wide variety of guided tours. Expect explosions and excitement at the stunt show, and be sure to check out the special-effects studio to find out how the seemingly impossible makes it onto the big screen. At Bullyversum, German film director and actor Michael "Bully" Herbig welcomes every visitor (almost) personally. The 4D experience cinema (children taller than 1.2 m/4 ft only) should not be missed *(see p54)*.

7 BMW Welt

A surefire hit with car-obsessed little ones, BMW's mega showroom lets you get behind the wheel of high-powered models, find out how a petrol engine works and watch motorbike riders perform stunts on the steps and floor space. There's also a café and a shop (see p129).

8 Sea Life

MAP E1 ■ Willi-Daume-Platz 1 ■ (089) 450000 ■ Open 10am–7pm daily ■ Adm ■ www.visitsealife.com

Many of the creatures at this aquarium within the Olympiapark are on the Red List of Threatened Species. The seahorses and touch pool are firm favourites with kids, while everyone enjoys feeding time (see p33).

Shark tunnel, Seaworld

9 Schauburg

Housed in a former cinema, this theatre for children puts on around 350 performances a year, all in German (see p53).

10 Wildpark Poing

Osterfeldweg 20, Poing ■ (081) 2180617 ■ Open Apr–Oct: 9am–5pm daily Nov–Mar; until 4pm ■ www.wildpark-poing.net

A circular route guides visitors on a journey of discovery featuring native species, enclosures and aviaries in a simulated natural habitat. There's the opportunity to pet and feed some of the animals, and birds of prey shows take place in summer.

CHILD-FRIENDLY CAFÉS AND RESTAURANTS

Café Zuckertag

1 Café Zuckertag
MAP L6 ■ Ehrengutstraße 10
Enjoy breakfast, lunch or cake while the little ones have fun in the playroom.

2 Seehaus
Seehaus on the Kleinhesseloher See has boats for hire (see p23).

3 Café de Bambini
MAP G2 ■ Marktstraße 7
Enjoy a coffee while clothes shopping for the kids. Little ones can play in the fun zone or tuck into baby food.

4 Chinesischer Turm
A nostalgic carousel can be found right next to the beer garden (see p23).

5 Aumeister
Sondermeierstraße 1
This beer garden in the northern part of the Englischer Garten has its own adventure playground.

6 Turncafé
MAP E3 ■ Hiltenspergerstraße 43
A play area and activity room are available for tiny tots.

7 Kaiser Otto
MAP M5 ■ Westermühlstraße 8
Childminders are on hand to help in the Kids Lounge for brunch (Sat and Sun 10am–2pm).

8 Hofbräukeller
MAP Q4 ■ Innere Wiener Straße 19
This large play area offers supervision for children aged 8 and under (noon–8pm Mon–Fri, 10am–8pm Sat and Sun).

9 Vits
MAP N4 ■ Rumfordstraße 49
This popular coffee roasting house has a cosy family corner.

10 Hirschau
MAP H2 ■ Gyßlingstraße 15
The beer garden here has the perfect view of the fenced play park.

TOP 10 Theatre, Concerts and Opera

The Philharmonic Hall at Gasteig

1 Gasteig

An unwieldy brick structure on the outside, this cultural centre hosts over 1,800 events per year – from concerts by the Munich Philharmonic to the city's Filmfest. The Philharmonic Hall offers seating for 2,500 and is complemented by other smaller auditoriums (see p112).

2 Residenztheater

In 1951, the Neues Residenztheater opened its doors next to the opera house. The "Resi" puts on a wide range of productions across its venues, which include the Cuvilliés-Theater and Marstall (see p89).

Performance of *The Government Inspector* at the Residenztheater

3 Bavarian State Opera

Run by artistic director Nikolaus Bachler and general musical director Kirill Petrenko, the opera house at the national theatre draws in half a million visitors every year to over 400 performances (see p89).

4 Herkulessaal

MAP N3 ■ Residenzstraße 1 (Hofgarten entrance) ■ (089) 290671

This vast hall within the Residenz hosts a diverse range of concerts, from orchestral pieces to chamber music performances.

5 Prinzregententheater

MAP R3 ■ Prinzregentenplatz 12 ■ (089) 2185 1970 ■ www.theaterakademie.de

Built in 1901 as a Wagner festival theatre, the space – conceived as an amphitheatre – is chiefly used as a performance venue for the Bayerische Theaterakademie August Everding.

6 Münchner Volkstheater

MAP L2 ■ Brienner Straße 50 ■ (089) 5234655 ■ www.muenchner-volkstheater.de

Theatregoers come here for a sophisticated repertoire of entertaining, popular plays.

7 Cuvilliés-Theater

Munich's most elaborate and historically significant theatre, which underwent substantial renovations around ten years ago, is used for performances by the Bayerische Staatstheater and occasionally for other musical events (see p17).

8 Münchner Kammerspiele

MAP N3 ■ Maximilianstraße 28
■ (089) 23 396600 ■ www.muenchner-kammerspiele.de
Built by Richard Riemerschmid in 1901, this theatre – considered one of the best stages in Germany – became the home of the Münchner Kammerspiele. It caused a stir in the 1920s by staging the works of Bertolt Brecht.

Deutsches Theater at night

9 Deutsches Theater

MAP L3–4 ■ Schwanthalerstraße 13 ■ (089) 55234444
■ www.deutsches-theater.de
The German Theatre is the main venue for hit international musicals, such as *Cats*, *Grease*, *Evita* and *West Side Story*, all translated into German, of course.

10 Staatstheater am Gärtnerplatz

MAP N5 ■ Gärtnerplatz 3 ■ www.staatstheateramgaertnerplatz.de
Built in 1865 as a bourgeois equivalent to the royal theatre houses, this intimate theatre hosts operas, operettas and musicals. It opened in late 2017 after renovation.

SMALL STAGES AND CABARETS

Metropoltheater, a former cinema

1 Pasinger Fabrik
August-Exter-Straße 1, München-Pasing ■ (089) 82 929079
Theatre and opera in the cultural centre.

2 Komödie im Bayerischen Hof
MAP M3 ■ Promenadeplatz 6
■ (089) 292810
Comedies and revues.

3 HochX
MAP N6 ■ Entenbachstraße 37
■ (089) 2097 0321
Dance, performance, video art, etc.

4 TamS-Theater
MAP G2 ■ Haimhauserstraße 13a
■ (089) 345890
Unusual productions since 1970.

5 Teamtheater
MAP N4 ■ Am Einlass 2a and 4
■ (089) 260 4333 or 260 6636
Independent theatre with two zones: "Tankstelle" & "Salon".

6 Schauburg
MAP F3 ■ Elisabethplatz ■ (089) 2333 7155 ■ www.schauburg.net
A renowned stage for young people.

7 Blutenburgtheater
MAP D3 ■ Blutenburgstraße 35
■ (089) 123 4300
A mystery production venue.

8 Metropoltheater
Floriansmühlstraße 5, Freimann
■ (089) 32 195533
An exceptional alternative theatre.

9 Lach- und Schießgesellschaft
MAP G2 ■ Ursulastraße 9 ■ (089) 391997
Political cabaret with bite.

10 Theater im Fraunhofer
MAP M5 ■ Fraunhoferstraße 9
■ (089) 267850
Small stage for everything from music to cabaret.

The Bavarian Hollywood

Bavaria Filmstadt: the popular Bullyversum attraction

1 Bavaria Filmstadt and Bullyversum

Bavariafilmplatz 7, Geiselgasteig ▪ (089) 64 992000 ▪ Open 9am–2:30 or 4:30pm daily (depending on tour) ▪ www.filmstadt.de

Munich's suburb of Geiselgasteig has been a centre for film-making since 1910. Major productions have been shot here, among them Wolfgang Petersen's *Das Boot* and films by Rainer Werner Fassbinder and Ingmar Bergman. Bavaria Filmstadt runs guided tours, and the latest attraction is "Bullyversum", inspired by comic and director Michael Herbig, complete with hands-on audience participation *(see p50)*.

Poster for Filmfest München

2 Hochschule für Fernsehen und Film München

MAP M2 ▪ Bernd-Eichinger-Platz 1 ▪ (089) 689570 ▪ www.hff-muenchen.de

The HFF (University of Television and Film Munich) has been a training ground for film-makers since 1967, and graduates of this prestigious institute include Wim Wenders and Roland Emmerich. The venue hosts screenings in summer.

3 Filmfest München

Since 1983, the largest German public film festival has been screening the latest international films at the end of June. The Gasteig *(see p112)* is the festival hub, with screenings held at cinemas throughout the city. An offshoot of the festival, the International Festival of Film Academies (Filmschoolfest Munich) takes place in November.

4 Filmmuseum München

MAP M4 ▪ St-Jakobs-Platz 1 ▪ (089) 23 396450 (tickets) ▪ shows 6:30 and 9pm Tue–Sun (Thu 7pm) ▪ DA ▪ www.muenchner-stadtmuseum.de

This theatre is equipped with the latest projection technology for all film formats. For over 40 years, it has been screening foreign films, film series, films from the museum's own archives, and silent movie reconstructions (often with live music accompaniment).

5 DOK.fest München

May is the month of documentary film for Munich's cinemas, with three popular competitions. The festival also serves as a get-together for those in the industry.

6 Fantasy Filmfest

A penchant for genre cinema is a prerequisite for this festival of non-mainstream films, from horror to thrillers and sci-fi (Aug/Sep).

7 Mathäser

MAP L3 ■ Bayerstraße 3–5 ■ (089) 515651 ■ DA ■ www. mathaeser.de

A modern multiplex cinema, which is also used for film premieres.

8 Open-Air Cinemas

If you're looking to enjoy a film in the great outdoors during the summer, head to Olympiapark, Westpark, Viehhof or Königsplatz.

Open-air cinema, Olympiapark

9 Arri Kino

MAP N1 ■ Türkenstraße 91 ■ (089) 38 899664 ■ www.arri-kino.de

Named for the Arri movie camera company, this cinema, complete with a large foyer area and bar, is rich in tradition.

10 Werkstattkino

MAP M5 ■ Fraunhoferstraße 9 ■ (089) 2 607250 ■ DA ■ www.werkstattkino.de

Tucked away in the basement of a rear courtyard building, this cinema is dedicated to screening films outside the mainstream, which are often shown in their original languages.

MUNICH FILM-MAKERS

Rainer-W.-Fassbinder-Platz

1 Percy Adlon
This director (b. 1935) worked in Hollywood following the unexpected success of *Out of Rosenheim*.

2 Herbert Achternbusch
Born in Munich in 1938, this agent provocateur known for film, writing and painting, creates anarchic Bavarian films.

3 The Verhoevens
Michael Verhoeven (b. 1938) belongs to a prominent family of actors and directors, and is married to actress Senta Berger.

4 Joseph Vilsmaier
This successful director (b. 1939) is famous for his biopics, such as *Comedian Harmonists* (1997).

5 Helmut Dietl
Dietl (1944–2015) portrayed the Munich scene in TV series such as *Monaco Franze* (1983) and *Kir Royal* (1985).

6 Rainer Werner Fassbinder
Famous prodigy of the New German Cinema, Fassbinder (1945–82) directed more than 40 films.

7 May Spils
With her 1967 *Zur Sache Schätzchen (To the Point, Darling)*, Spils created the film that captured the spirit of Schwabing.

8 Doris Dörrie
Since rising to fame with her 1985 film *Männer*, director and author Dörrie (b. 1955) has won numerous awards.

9 Caroline Link/Dominik Graf
In 2002, Link (b. 1964) won the Oscar for Best Foreign Film for *Nirgendwo in Afrika*. She lives in Munich with fellow director, Dominik Graf (b. 1952).

10 Florian Gallenberger
Gallenberger (b. 1972) won an Oscar in 2001 for his short film *Quiero ser*.

🔟 Nightlife

Dancefloor at indie club Strom

① Strom
MAP K6 ▪ Lindwurmstraße 88
▪ From 10pm Fri and Sat
▪ www.strom-muc.de

From parties to concerts, indie fans are right at home in this club on Lindwurmhof, which offers a programme of DJ extravaganzas.

② Bob Beaman
 straße 4/Amalienstraße corner
▪ From midnight Fri and Sat
▪ www.bobbeamanclub.com

Bob Beaman doesn't simply host first-rate DJs, it also boasts exceptional acoustics and an impressive sound system: a treat for the ears with quality bookings from across Europe.

③ Paradiso Tanzbar
 MAP N4 ▪ Rumfordstraße 2
▪ From 10pm Fri and Sat
▪ www.paradiso-tanzbar.de

In the rooms of the once-legendary "Old Mrs Henderson" club, which welcomed the likes of Mick Jagger, David Bowie and Freddie Mercury, the Paradiso is now making a mark of its own. A popular club in retro 1980s style, complete with flashing dance floor and classic retro hits.

④ Muffathalle and Ampere
MAP P4 ▪ Zellstraße 4
▪ www.muffatwerk.de

The Muffathalle, the smaller Ampere, and the colonnaded café, are open only for scheduled events, such as parties, concerts, theatre, productions, dance recitals and readings. This former heating plant is one of the most beautiful venues in the city, located right behind the Müller'sches Volksbad. The beer garden is inviting on a sunny day.

⑤ Harry Klein
 MAP L3 ▪ Sonnenstraße 8
▪ From 8pm Thu, 10pm Fri and Sat
▪ www.harrykleinclub.de

Harry Klein is one of a number of clubs on Sonnenstraße that have popped up in the past few years. DJ sets here range from techno house to electro, and the lighting concept creates an exciting vibe.

Bob Beaman – the best sound quality in Munich

6 P1
MAP P2 ▪ Prinzregentenstraße 1 ▪ From 11pm Mon–Sat ▪ www.p1-club.de

P1 (named after its address) was once a well-known hang-out of the FC Bayern players, with a reputation reaching far beyond Munich. The celebrities have now largely moved on and the atmosphere is a little more chilled. Great sound quality.

7 Rote Sonne
MAP M3 ▪ Maximiliansplatz 5 ▪ From 10pm Fri and Sat ▪ www.rote-sonne.com

Techno and electro are the genres of choice at this funky little club on Maximiliansplatz, which hosts live gigs during the week.

Rote: small size, big atmosphere

8 Pacha
MAP M3 ▪ Maximiliansplatz 5 ▪ From 6:30pm Thu, 11pm Fri and Sat ▪ www.pacha-muenchen.de

This club offers the full range of house music and hosts top DJs. The outdoor terrace is a treat in summer.

9 089 Bar
MAP M3 ▪ Maximiliansplatz 5 ▪ From 9pm Tue–Sat ▪ www.089-bar.de

This club on Maximiliansplatz with a central bar and dance floor is open until the early hours.

10 Cord Club
MAP L4 ▪ Sonnenstraße 18 ▪ From 8:30, 10 or 11pm Mon, Fri & Sat ▪ www.cord-muenchen.de

DJs, live acts and themed nights await visitors to Cord. Great views of Sonnenstraße from the windows.

GAY AND LESBIAN VENUES

1 Deutsche Eiche
MAP N4 ▪ Reichenbachstraße 13 ▪ www.deutsche-eiche.de
A well-established gay pub with a hotel and sauna.

2 Café Nil
MAP M5 ▪ Hans-Sachs-Straße 2 ▪ www.cafenil.com
One of Munich's first gay cafés.

3 Café Glück
MAP M6 ▪ Palmstraße 4 ▪ www.cafe-glueck.com
Light bites, drinks, cakes and music.

4 Jennifer Parks
MAP M5 ▪ Holzstraße 14 ▪ www.jennifer-parks.com
LGBT-friendly; quiz nights and parties.

5 Melcher's
MAP N4 ▪ Buttermelcherstraße 21 ▪ www.das-melchers.de
This restaurant is a popular choice with lesbians.

6 NY.Club
MAP L4 ▪ Sonnenstraße 25 ▪ www.nyclub.de
Sophisticated gay disco on Fri and Sat.

7 Edelheiss
MAP M4 ▪ Pestalozzistraße 6 ▪ www.edelheiss.de
Second beer free on Thursdays (8–10pm) if you have a beard.

8 Café im Sub
MAP M4 ▪ Müllerstraße 14 ▪ www.subonline.org
Gay communication centre and café.

9 Bau
MAP M5 ▪ Müllerstraße 41 ▪ www.bau-munich.de
Great bar for fans of denim, leather, rubber and uniforms.

10 CSD
▪ www.csdmuenchen.de
Pride Week (early July) involves a parade, street party and club night.

Deutsche Eiche

🔟 **Bavarian Dishes**

Bratwürst with Kraut

① Wurst and Würstl

In Bavaria, *Wurst* (sausage) is eaten as part of a cold snack known as *Brotzeit* ("bread time"). A regional speciality is *Weißwurst* (boiled veal sausage), which is cooked in boiling water and peeled out of its skin before being enjoyed with sweet mustard. Typical hot sausage dishes include *Schweinswürstl* (Franconian pork sausages) served with sauerkraut or *Leberkäse* (meat loaf). *Regensburger* (boiled sausages) are the star of the show in any self-respecting Bavarian *Wurstsalat* (sausage salad).

② Münchner Schnitzel

The Wittelsbachs were related to the Habsburgs, and so many of the dishes commonly found in Bavaria were originally inspired by Bohemian Austrian cuisine, for example *Knödel* (dumplings),

Münchner Schnitzel: a savoury treat

Mehlspeisen (pastries) and even schnitzel. The Munich twist on schnitzel includes a horseradish, sweet mustard and *Breznbrösel* (pretzel breadcrumb) coating.

③ Schweinebraten

Succulent *Schweinebraten* (roast pork) is a real Bavarian favourite. The local way to cook it involves scoring the rind before putting the joint into the oven to roast. The meat is then continuously basted with beer (ideally dark lager) while it is roasting, until the rind develops into crispy crackling. *Schweinebraten* is traditionally served with *Knödeln* and sauerkraut or coleslaw.

④ Knödel

Dumplings are a mainstay of Bavarian cooking. Originally a means of using up leftover, stale bread rolls, by soaking them, *Semmelknödel* are particularly popular. A tasty alternative is the *Breznknödel*, made with stale *Laugenbrezel* (lye pretzels). Another type is *Kartoffelknödel*, made from grated potatoes with a toasted cube of white bread in the centre. Dumplings that are made exclusively from cooked potatoes are also sometimes used for making sweet pastries, such as *Zwetschgenknödel* (plum dumplings).

Plain salted pretzels

5 Kässpätzle
A type of soft egg noodle, *Spätzle* originated in the Swabia region. The cooking method involves scraping the almost runny *Spätzle* dough into boiling water. The end product is available in a variety of different versions and dishes. One dish, known as *Allgäuer Kässpätzle*, involves cheese and minced onions.

Aubergine dish

6 Steckerlfisch
Anyone who's been to Oktoberfest will be more than familiar with the smell of this fish on a stick – typically trout, char or mackerel – cooked on a charcoal grill.

7 Brezn and Semmeln
The *Laugenbrezn* is the region's most popular and common type of pretzel, and its appeal sky-rockets during Oktoberfest. *Semmel* is the Bavarian name for a bread roll.

8 Obatzda
This spreadable cheese (made from Camembert, butter, quark, paprika and onion) is a beer-garden favourite.

9 Süßspeisen
Bavarian *Süßspeisen* or desserts are typically hearty. Favourites include *Apfelstrudel* (apple strudel), *Hollerkücherl* (elderflower pancakes), *Dampfnudeln* (steamed dumplings) and Austrian *Kaiserschmarrn* (shredded pancakes), often served with fruit compote.

10 Gebäck
The Bavarian region is home to a whole host of *Gebäck* (pastries). Anyone with a sweet tooth should look out for *Zwetschgendatschi* (plum cake), *Rohrnudeln* (sweet filled rolls made from yeast dough), and the ever-popular *Auszogne* (doughnuts).

VEGETARIAN AND VEGAN

1 Prinz Myshkin
Munich's top vegetarian restaurant serves imaginative and flavour-packed meat-free and vegan dishes. *(see p83)*.

2 Max Pett
MAP M4 ▪ Pettenkoferstraße 8
This place serves a vegan twist on Wiener Schnitzel. No alcohol.

3 Café Ignaz
MAP F3 ▪ Georgenstraße 67
An extensive menu featuring crêpes, gnocchi and organic beer.

4 Gratitude
MAP N1 ▪ Türkenstraße 55
This organic restaurant offers vegan, gluten-free and raw dishes.

5 Bodhi
MAP J4 ▪ Ligsalzstraße 23
Vegan Bavarian-style restaurant serving *Obatzda* and schnitzel burgers.

6 Vegelangelo
MAP P4 ▪ Thomas-Wimmer-Ring 15
The vegetarian food here packs a real punch, from the pasta creations to truffle risotto.

7 Tian
MAP N4 ▪ Frauenstraße 4
This restaurant by Viktualienmarkt offers meat-free delights with a gourmet feel.

8 Deli Kitchen
MAP L2 ▪ Augustenstraße 5
A vegan shop with its own small stylish restaurant.

9 Tushita Teehaus
MAP M5 ▪ Klenzestraße 53
Great teas and fresh vegan snacks.

10 Lost Weekend
MAP N1 ▪ Schellingstraße 3
A popular bookshop café serving vegan coffee and cake.

Meat-free appetizer, Prinz Myshkin

🔟 Restaurants

1 Vinaiolo
MAP Q5 ▪
Steinstraße 42
▪ (089) 48 950356
▪ Closed Sat lunch ▪
www.vinaiolo.de ▪ €€€
This Haidhausen restaurant has a nostalgic shop-style interior and represents the perfect blend of an osteria, a bistro and a wine cellar. Guests can expect to enjoy inspired Italian cuisine along with accompanying wines (at reasonable prices). Good-value lunchtime menus and a four-course evening menu are available.

2 Tantris
Boasting two Michelin stars, Tantris has long been one of the best restaurants in Germany. Hans Haas has been at the helm since 1991, and his philosophy of inspiring culinary experiences is unrivalled. There are tasting menus as well as à la carte and guests have no fewer than three sommeliers to call upon during their meal. This is the perfect venue for celebrating a special occasion – not least due to its bold, retro decor, which almost steals the show from the food (see p109).

Zauberberg's bright dining room

3 Zauberberg
MAP D3 ▪ Hedwigstraße 14
▪ (089) 18 999178 ▪ Closed Sun–Tue, lunch ▪ www.restaurant-zauberberg.de ▪ €€€
Zauberberg is renowned for creating innovative dishes from fresh, seasonal ingredients. An early-bird three-course menu (€33) is available from 6 to 7pm on Wednesdays and Thursdays. This bright, friendly eatery also has outdoor seating.

4 Pageou
MAP N3 ▪ Kardinal-Faulhaber-Straße 10 ▪ (089) 24 231310 ▪ Closed Sun and Mon ▪ www.pageou.de ▪ €€€
Ali Güngörmüş, whose restaurant Le Canard Nouveau (now closed) won a Michelin star, serves modern cuisine with an oriental twist at this restaurant in the Fünf Höfe shopping centre. The dining area has its own gallery on a mezzanine level for smaller groups, as well as an inner courtyard terrace.

5 Landersdorfer and Innerhofer
MAP M4 ▪ Hackenstraße 6–8 ▪ (089) 26 018637 ▪ Closed Sat and Sun ▪ www.landersdorferundinnerhofer.de ▪ €€€
Hans Landersdorfer's Austrian-inspired menu is a pure delight. Wine recommendations are provided by Robert Innerhofer, and there is a two-course lunch menu for €25.

Retro interior at Tantris

6 Matsuhisa Munich
MAP N3 ▪ Neuturmstraße 1
▪ (089) 29098 1875 ▪ www.
mandarinoriental.com ▪ €€€

The only restaurant in Germany
headed by top chef Nobu Matsuhisa
can be found in Munich's Mandarin
Oriental hotel. The fusion of
Japanese and Peruvian cuisine
might not come cheap, but it's
definitely worth it.

7 Königshof
Karte L3 ▪ Karlsplatz 25
▪ (089) 551 366138 ▪ Closed Sun and
Mon ▪ www.koenigshof-muenchen.
de ▪ €€€

Königshof is on the first floor of the
eponymous hotel, offering a view of
Stachus. Here Martin Fauster cooks
up the finest cuisine in his Michelin-
starred restaurant.

Formal decor at Königshof

8 Geisel's Vinothek
MAP L3 ▪ Schützenstraße 11
▪ (089) 5 5137 7140 ▪ Sun evenings
only ▪ www.excelsior-hotel.de ▪ €€€

The Vinothek at the Hotel Excelsior
has a 500-bottle wine list to
complement the kitchen's
sophisticated cuisine.

9 Südtiroler Stuben
MAP N3 ▪ Am Platzl 8 ▪ (089)
2166900 ▪ Closed Sun ▪ www.
schuhbeck.de ▪ €€€

Upmarket Bavarian–Mediterranean cuisine awaits guests at
Alfons Schuhbeck's gastro temple.

10 Rue des Halles
The oldest French restaurant
in Munich offers classic cooking at
its finest *(see p117)*.

BREAKFAST AND BRUNCH

White Rabbit's Room

1 White Rabbit's Room
MAP Q5 ▪ Franziskanerstraße 19
▪ www.white-rabbits-room.de
Quaint café with great croissants.

2 Vorstadt-Café
MAP N1 ▪ Türkenstraße 83
▪ www.vorstadt-cafe.de
Café with outdoor seating near
the university.

3 Café im Müller'schen Volksbad
MAP P4 ▪ Rosenheimer Straße 1
▪ www.cafe-volksbad.de
Art Nouveau-style café at the
Müller'sches Volksbad.

4 Das Neuhausen
MAP D3 ▪ Blutenburgstraße 106
▪ www.dasneuhausen.de
Great breakfast selection.

5 Café Altschwabing
MAP M1 ▪ Schellingstraße 56
▪ www.altschwabing.com
Stucco decor, coffee-house ambience.

6 Aroma Kaffeebar
MAP M5 ▪ Pestalozzistraße 24
▪ www.aromakaffeebar.com
Breakfast, coffee and home-made cake
served all day long.

7 Café am Beethovenplatz
Breakfast with live music (Sunday from
11am), and a popular terrace *(see p123)*.

8 Café Noel
MAP Q5 ▪ Metzstraße 8
Delicious cakes, sandwiches, light bites
and a cosy atmosphere.

9 Tagträumer
MAP L6 ▪ Dreimühlenstraße 17
▪ www.tagtraum-muenchen.de
Fabulous weekend breakfasts.

10 Stenz
MAP K5 ▪ Lindwurmstraße 122
Breakfast with a Bavarian twist.

For a key to Restaurant price ranges see p83

🔟 Bars and Cafés

① Zephyr Bar
MAP N5 ■ Baaderstraße 68
■ Closed Sun

This bar, a popular hang-out in the Glockebach quarter, might not look much from the outside, but step through its doors and prepare to be wowed with spectacular drinks. Their motto: "Drinking is a necessity – enjoy it as an art form."

② Juleps
MAP R5 ■ Breisacher Straße 18
■ (089) 4480044

Laid-back, American-style place, where you can enjoy one of the bartenders' 200 different cocktails or simply prop up the bar with a beer straight from the bottle. As for food, the menu ranges from lobster through to Tex-Mex.

③ Bar Centrale
MAP N4 ■ Ledererstraße 23
■ (089) 223762

At this Italian all-day bar and lounge, take a seat towards the front (or at one of the tables outside) and enjoy the tantalizing aroma of espresso. Head further into the bar and you'll find yourself transported back to the 1960s. Great cocktails and pasta.

④ Café Frischhut
MAP N4 ■ Prälat-Zistl-Straße 8
■ (089) 268237

While hungover revellers once flocked to this café from as early as 5am, it now opens around 8am. It is also known as "Schmalznudel" after its popular fresh pastries and buns.

The cosy interior of Flushing Meadows

⑤ Flushing Meadows
MAP M5 ■ Fraunhoferstraße 32
■ (089) 55 279170

The rooftop bar of this hotel in the Glockenbach quarter offers magnificent views of the old town. If you're lucky, you can even see as far as the Alps on a clear day. The drinks menu is a mix of German specialities and international favourites.

⑥ Gamsbar
MAP N2 ■ Brienner Straße 10
■ (089) 225004 ■ Closed Sun

Munich at its eccentric best: enjoy a spot of shopping at Ed Meier then head for a drink at Gamsbar. With its sophisticated interior and alpine details, this bar is more of a daytime or early evening venue, serving coffee, bar food and cocktails.

Pastries and buns for breakfast at the Café Frischhut

The owner was once purveyor to the royal Bavarian court and is keen to create a refined atmosphere with a hint of kitsch.

7 Schumann's
MAP N2 ■ Odeonsplatz 6–7 ■ (089) 229060

Charles Schumann has been running this legendary bar for 30 years. In a city where fashionable spots come and go, this bar has always been popular with famous and not-so-famous visitors alike. It even survived the big move from Maximilianstraße to its present location on Odeonsplatz. The first-floor bar, Les Fleurs du Mal, has a 9-m (30-ft) long table where guests can discuss drinks with the bartender, and there's a gorgeous terrace looking out towards the Hofgarten.

8 Café Lotti
An attractive café with pretty pastel decor, located near the Pinakotheken, this place serves great breakfasts (see p101).

The pastel pink Café Lotti

9 Stereo Café
MAP N3 ■ Residenzstraße 25 ■ (089) 24 210243 ■ Closed Sun

This coffee shop offers freshly roasted coffee, cake and light bites, all with a great view of the Residenz.

10 Café Hüller
MAP N5 ■ Eduard-Schmid-Straße 8 ■ (089) 1893 8713

Breakfast here comes highly recommended, whether you opt for something sweet, hearty or healthy. The daily menu includes soups, vegetarian dishes and desserts.

BARS AND CAFÉS WITH LIVE MUSIC

1 Jazzbar Vogler
MAP N4 ■ Rumfordstraße17 ■ (089) 294662
Blues nights, jazz concerts and readings.

2 Waldwirtschaft Großhesselohe
Georg-Kalb-Straße 3, PullachGroß-hesselohe ■ (089) 74 994030
Popular pub staging live jazz concerts.

3 Café am Beethovenplatz
Munich's oldest café with live classical music and jazz (see p123).

4 Antons
St-Martin-Straße 7 ■ (089) 6973 7245
Restaurant and bar with live music on Saturdays.

5 Night Club
MAP M3 ■ Promenadeplatz 2–6 ■ (089) 212 0994
The cellar in the Bayerischer Hof plays host to live acts from funk to jazz.

6 Irish Folk Pub
MAP G2 ■ Giselastraße 11 ■ (089) 342446
Serves up Irish stew, Guinness, whiskey and live Irish folk music every Thursday.

7 Jazzclub Unterfahrt
MAP Q4 ■ Einsteinstraße 42 ■ (089) 448 2794
A jazz club at the Einstein Kultur centre

8 Wirtshaus zum Isartal
■ Brudermühlstraße 2 ■ (089) 772121
A rustic tavern with a stage for plays and small productions as well as live music.

9 Kaffee Giesing
Tegernseer Landstraße 96 ■ (089) 692 0579
A cult pub with live music, founded by songwriter Konstantin Wecker.

10 Hofbräuhaus
If you like brass band music, you'll be in your element at the Hofbräuhaus (see p89).

Jazzclub Unterfahrt

🔟 Beer Gardens

Chinesischer Turm

1 Chinesischer Turm

MAP Q1 ▪ **Englischer Garten**
▪ **7,000 capacity** ▪ **Play area, old wooden carousel nearby**

The Chinese Tower is one of the city's most famous landmarks, and is frequented by students, tourists and locals alike *(see p23)*. Brass bands play on the first floor of the pagoda at the weekend.

2 Taxisgarten

Karte C2 ▪ **Taxisstraße 12**
▪ **1,500 capacity**

This neighbourhood beer garden in Neuhausen is a cosy spot sheltered by chestnut and ash trees.

Taxisgarten sign

3 Augustiner-Keller

MAP K2 ▪ **Arnulfstraße 52**
▪ **5,000 capacity (2,500 with table service)** ▪ **Play area**

This vast beer garden shaded by ancient chestnut trees near a former place of execution has been in operation since the 19th century. Two hundred decorated tables for the regulars add a whimsical note. On warm summer evenings, this beer garden is packed. Don't miss the Augustiner Edelstoff on tap from wooden barrels.

4 Seehaus

MAP G2 ▪ **Englischer Garten**
▪ **2,500 capacity (400 on the terrace)**
▪ **Play area, lakeside boat hire**

A great place to people-watch, this popular beer garden is at the centre of the Englischer Garten, right on the Kleinhesseloher See. The terrace is stylish, while the beer garden (serving Paulaner) has a cosy atmosphere *(see p23)*.

5 Hofbräukeller

MAP Q4 ▪ **Innere Wiener Straße 19** ▪ **1,400 capacity (400 with table service)** ▪ **Play area**

Across the Isar in Haidhausen, the Hofbräukeller – once the site of a brewery and its cellar – has been serving beer since 1892. The canopy of chestnuts is so dense that drinkers remain dry and comfortable even on damp days.

6 Hirschgarten

Munich's largest beer garden (8,000 capacity) can be found right next to Schloss Nymphenburg. Augustiner Edelstoff is served on tap from the huge wooden barrel, known as a "Hirsch" *(see p128)*.

7 Aumeister

Sondermeier-straße 1 ▪ **3,000 capacity**
▪ **Adventure playground**

This huge beer garden on the north side of the Englischer Garten serves

Foaming Bavarian beers

Hofbräu, along with a selection of seasonal beers, including Starkbier in March, and Sommerbier and Wiesnbier during Oktoberfest. Parasols shelter drinkers on the Mediterranean terrace.

Drinkers at the Viktualienmarkt

8 Biergarten am Viktualienmarkt

MAP N4 ■ Viktualienmarkt 9 ■ 800 capacity (200 catered to with table service)

Nestled between the market stalls of Viktualienmarkt, this beer garden is about as central as it gets. What's extra special about this place is that it serves beer from all of Munich's breweries on a six-week rotation. In the summer months, it hosts concerts by traditional bands on Sundays, and the Brunnenfest takes place on the first Friday in August under the watchful eye of the statue of the actor Weiß Ferdl in a fountain.

9 Wirtshaus am Bavariapark

Chestnut trees shelter this beer garden in Bavariapark with capacity for 1,200 patrons (and a further 300 on the terrace). Serves Augustiner (see p125).

10 Zum Flaucher

MAP E6 ■ Isarauen 8 ■ 700 capacity ■ Play area

This idyllic beer garden on the banks of the Isar is dotted with beautiful old trees. You're likely to come across sunbathers on the Isar beach, as well as cyclists and families with children. Serves Löwenbräu.

TRADITIONS IN AND AROUND MUNICH

1 Schäfflertanz
Munich, Carnival
This dance of the Schäffler takes place every seven years (next in 2019) to commemorate the end of the plague.

2 Tanz der Marktfrauen
Munich, Shrove Tuesday
Women on the stalls at Viktualienmarkt dance in fantastic costumes.

3 Starkbierzeit
Bavaria, St Joseph's Day (19 March) until Easter
Celebrating the "fifth season of the year" by tapping barrels of potent Starkbier.

4 Maibaum
Bavaria, 1 May
The day to set up the maypole.

5 Fronleichnamsprozession
Thursday after Trinity Sunday
Processions for the Feast of Corpus Christi take place across South Bavaria, the largest running through Munich.

6 Kocherlball
Third Sun in July
Costumed couples dance the Ländler, Zwiefacher and Polka to pay homage to the servants who once did the same.

7 Leonhardi-Umzüge
Upper Bavaria, first Sunday in November
Processions in honour of St Leonhard, patron saint of horses.

8 Christkindlmärkte
Bavaria, first day of advent until 24 Dec
Christmas markets in Marienplatz.

9 Alphornblasen, Jodeln and Schuhplatteln
Alphorns, yodelling and the thigh-slapping Schuhplatteln dance.

10 Trachten
Witness local costumes (Trachten) in the region's processions and festivals.

Horses in the Leonhardi-Umzug

🔟 Traditional Taverns

The façade of the Franziskaner Fuchsenstuben

1 Franziskaner Fuchsenstuben

MAP N3 ■ Perusastraße 5
■ (089) 2318120 ■ €–€€

This 200-year-old traditional pub is said to serve the best *Leberkäse* (meat loaf) in town. The *Weißwürste* (sausages) are highly recommended too.

2 Hofbräuhaus

You can't come to Munich and not pay a visit to the most famous beer hall in the world *(see p89)*.

3 Spatenhaus an der Oper

MAP N3 ■ Residenzstraße 12
■ (089) 2907060 ■ €€

The ground floor of this traditional pub on Max-Joseph-Platz has a homely, unpretentious atmosphere, while the upper floor has a more sophisticated ambience. Diners come here to enjoy a menu of hearty Munich cooking.

4 Schneider Bräuhaus

The former Weiße Bräuhaus offers traditional Munich fare, including *Kronfleischküche* (skirt steak dishes). Whether you opt for *Kalbslüngerl* (pickled lights of veal), *Milzwurst* (spleen sausage) or *Schweinsbraten* (roast pork),

the food here is outstanding. A wheat bock beer called Aff is served on tap. Also, be sure to try the *Schneider Weisse (see p83)*.

5 Wirtshaus in der Au

MAP P5 ■ Lilienstraße 51
■ (089) 4481400 ■ €

The Wirtshaus, founded in 1901, is renowned for its dumplings, which include varieties containing either wild garlic, spinach or ham. Meat lovers might also want to try the duck, steak or ox fillet. Renowned dumpling-making courses are run by the owners for locals and visitors alike. Paulaner and Auer craft beer are served on tap.

Lion fountain, Hofbräuhaus

6 Zum Augustiner

Housed in a traditional building that operated as a brewery until 1885, this large restaurant has an interior that's well worth a look (particularly the mussel hall). In summer, there is outdoor seating in the paved pedestrian zone and in an arcaded courtyard *(see p83)*.

Outdoor tables at Zum Augustiner

7 Löwenbräukeller
MAP L2 ■ Stiglmaierplatz
■ (089) 54 726690 ■ €–€€

This historic building complete with exquisite taproom, ceremonial hall and a large beer garden dominates the Stiglmaierplatz. It also serves as a venue for carnival balls and congresses, and plays host to the tapping of the first Triumphator barrel to welcome in the "fifth season" in March. A stone lion, the Löwenbräu emblem, sits majestically above the entrance.

Main hall at the Löwenbräukeller

8 Paulaner Bräuhaus
A cosy, homely pub furnished with dark wood and brewing equipment. House-brewed Paulaner is, of course, served on tap. The game dishes in particular are excellent (see p125).

9 Fraunhofer
MAP M5 ■ Fraunhoferstraße 9
■ (089) 266460 ■ €

Parts of this atmospheric tavern date back to when it was first built, in around 1900. It attracts a mix of locals and tourists and hosts weekly music sessions on Sunday mornings. Its courtyard is home to both a cabaret stage and the legendary Werkstattkino cinema (see p55).

10 Augustiner Bräustuben
While Oktoberfest is in full swing, this is the place to come for a glimpse of the brewery's show horses. Both the inn itself and the brewery's stables are brimming with traditional Bavarian charm (see p125).

MUNICH AND BAVARIAN BEERS

1 Augustiner
Brewed since 1328 in the monastery near the cathedral, under the purity law since 1516, Augustiner is regarded as the champagne of beers.

2 Franziskaner Weissbier
Franciscan friars have brewed this beer since 1363 in the former monastery on Residenzstraße. Now part of the Spaten-Löwenbräu Group.

3 Paulaner
Pauline monks in the Au began to brew beer as far back as 1634. The most famous master brewer was Brother Barnabas, and Salvator beer is still made using his 18th-century recipe.

4 Löwenbräu
A traditional brew with a history going back to the 14th century. The largest brewery in Munich.

5 Hofbräu
Duke Wilhelm V founded his own court brewery in 1589. A new fermenting site was set up on Platzl in 1607 – it is now known as the Hofbräuhaus.

6 Spaten
This brewery is named after the 16th-century Spatt family.

7 Hacker-Pschorr
The first recorded mention of this beer was in 1417. Today, it is part of the Paulaner Group.

8 Erdinger Weißbier
Erdinger is one of the top sellers among nearly 1,000 differet types of Bavarian wheat beers.

9 Ayinger
This small brewery in Aying is home to a dozen well-known beers.

10 Andechser
Beer has been brewed at this Benedictine abbey on the "sacred mountain" since the Middle Ages.

Brewery maypole decorations at Viktualienmarkt

TOP10 Shopping

1 Theatinerstraße and Residenzstraße

MAP N3

Theatinerstraße begins at Marienhof, behind the Neues Rathaus. This shopping street is home to fashion boutiques, high-end stores and the Fünf Höfe shopping centre. If you're looking for luxury brands, head for Residenzstraße, which runs parallel to Theatinerstraße.

2 Fünf Höfe

MAP N3 ■ www.fuenfhoefe.de

Historic buildings and contemporary architecture, arcades, courtyards, shops, culture and fine gastronomy – this award-winning example of urban design by architects Herzog & de Meuron covers the area between Theatinerstraße, Kardinal-Faulhaber-Straße, Maffeistraße and Salvatorstraße.

3 Sendlinger Straße and Hofstatt

MAP M4 ■ www.hofstatt.info

Sendlinger Straße is one of the oldest shopping streets in Munich and has several traditional stores, although it is becoming increasingly chic. Its latest addition is Hofstatt, a shopping mall with popular chains, such as Abercrombie & Fitch, Gant, Mango and Calzedonia.

Beck department store, Marienplatz

4 Pedestrian Zone

MAP M3

Munich's central pedestrian zone stretches along Kaufingerstraße and Neuhauser Straße to Karlsplatz/Stachus. This is the busiest street in the whole city, with several places of interest interspersed among the retail frenzy.

5 Maximilianstraße and Maximilianhöfe

MAP N3 ■ www.maximilianhoefe.de

This elegant 19th-century boulevard between the Nationaltheater and Altstadtring is one of the most exclusive retail destinations in Europe. Armani, Bulgari and Gucci are just some of the names that beckon from this shopping street designed in the "Maximilianstil" of the era by Friedrich Bürklein. The Maximilianhöfe complex (including brands such as Gianfranco Ferré and Dolce & Gabbana) attracts shoppers with money to burn.

6 Around Viktualienmarkt

MAP N4

Worth a stroll whether you're shopping or not, Viktualienmarkt is surrounded by speciality stores of all sizes (see p80). Small antiques shops

The modern Hofstatt arcade

Shopping « **69**

and the largest organic supermarket in the city line the narrow streets leading to the Isartor. A shopping arcade runs in the direction of Rindermarkt and the Löwenturm.

⑦ Around the University
MAP N1

Bounded by the Amalienstraße, Schellingstraße, Türkenstraße and Adalbertstraße, the student quarter features not only the bookshops you might expect, but also chic boutiques, jewellery stores and trendy design shops.

⑧ Leopoldstraße and Hohenzollernstraße
MAP FG2–3

Starting from the top of Giselastraße, Schwabing's Leopoldstraße is lined with shops, restaurants and cafés. Stroll along the side streets on the left-hand side of the boulevard (heading away from the centre), especially Hohenzollernstraße, for a wide variety of shops.

⑨ Around Gärtnerplatz
MAP N4–5

In addition to its popular cafés, bars and restaurants, the scenic Gärtnerplatz quarter is home to a whole host of specialist shops, such as Blutsgeschwister with its own fashion line.

Blutsgeschwister in the Gärtnerplatz

⑩ Shopping Centres

Major shopping centres outside central Munich include the OEZ (Olympia-Einkaufszentrum), Pasing Arcaden by the S-Bahn station, Riem Arcaden in the exhibition city of Riem, and the Einkaufs-Center Neuperlach.

MARKETS AND FAIRS

Viktualienmarkt

1 Viktualienmarkt
Established in 1807, Viktualienmarkt *(see p80)* is a top destination for foodies.

2 Elisabethmarkt
MAP F3
This market on Elisabethplatz is the second largest in Munich.

3 Wiener Markt
MAP Q4
The old market stalls here are often used as a set for films and TV shows.

4 Großmarkthalle
MAP E6
Munich wholesale market is full of atmosphere.

5 Auer Dulten
MAP P6 ▪ Mariahilfplatz ▪ www.auerdult.de
Three nine-day fairs run from the end of April, July and mid-October.

6 Antikmärkte
Flohmarkt München Daglfing and the open-air flea market at the Zenith exhibition centre are both brimming with trash, treasures and antiques.

7 Trödelmärkte and Flohmärkte
The city's largest flea markets are the Riesen-Flohmarkt on Theresienwiese and Flohmarkt München-Riem.

8 Hinterhofflohmärkte
www.hofflohmaerkte.de/muenchen
Many districts across the city hold their own backyard jumble sales.

9 Weihnachtsmärkte
The largest Christmas market is held in Marienplatz. If you're looking for more atmosphere, try those in the Schwabing and Haidhausen districts.

10 Magdalenenfest
MAP H2 ▪ Hirschgarten
A small July folk festival, with a market.

Sport and Wellness

Boulderwelt München West: climbing walls to suit all levels

1 Bouldering
www.boulderwelt.de

Bouldering is a form of rock climbing performed without the use of ropes or harnesses. Munich has two large bouldering halls – Boulderwelt München Ost (Ostbahnhof) and München West (Neuaubing).

2 AOK Blade Night
www.greencity.de

Environmental organization Green City runs Munich's Blade Night, where roller-bladers meet up every Monday evening (May–Sep) from 7pm on three empty roads.

ALLIANZ ARENA

The Allianz Arena in Fröttmaning, northern Munich, was built for the 2006 World Cup and is used by the city's two professional football clubs. Designed by architects Herzog & de Meuron, it has a transparent façade that can be illuminated in numerous colours. Holding 66,000 spectators, the stadium includes an enormous food court. The stadium can be reached via U-Bahn line U6.

Allianz Arena

3 Rock Climbing
www.klettern-muenchen.de

Munich is an ideal spot for fans of climbing; after all, the Alps are practically on its doorstep. The city is home to a number of artificial climbing walls for practising on before heading into the great outdoors to try out a real rock face.

4 Jogging
www.mrrc.de

Munich boasts plentiful parks of all sizes that are perfect for jogging (see pp66–7). The most beautiful paths are to be found in the Englischer Garten and along the banks of the Isar. If you prefer not to jog on your own, contact local organization Roadrunners, which can put you in touch with a group of runners at your level.

5 Hiking
www.alpenverein.de

There are plenty of beautiful hiking trails in and around Munich that make for easy walking. If you prefer a more extreme challenge, take a trip to the nearby Alps for mountain hiking. For information on the best routes, contact an organization like the Deutscher Alpenverein.

6 Golf

www.muenchen-spielt-golf.de

Golf is popular in Munich and the surrounding area, so much so that golfers can choose from more than 40 golf courses dotted in and around the Bavarian capital.

7 Cycling
www.adfc-bayern.de

Home to one of the best cycling path networks in Europe, Munich has several green routes that you can follow without the nuisance of exhaust fumes and noise. Check with the ADFC (German Cyclist's Association) for a selection of cycling tours in and around Munich.

8 Water Sports
www.swm.de ■ www.muenchen.de/freizeit.html

Munich and the nearby lake regions are a haven in summer for anyone who enjoys swimming, rowing, sailing, windsurfing or canoeing. Destinations range from city swimming pools to quarry ponds, small, idyllic moor lakes and the great lakes of Upper Bavaria.

Wellness treatment at Sai Spa

9 Wellness
www.sai-spa.de

Munich has responded to the rising popularity of wellness and offers a wide range of facilities, from the day spa at the organic supermarket to the Blue Spa in Bayerischer Hof. The Turkish bath at the Mathildenbad is hugely popular, while for an Asian-style ambience, Sai Spa is another good choice

10 Winter Sports
www.winter-muenchen.de

The city and its environs are a Mecca for winter sports fans, whether you like skiing, ice skating, snow-boarding, curling or sledging. With such a wide variety of winter sports, there's something for everyone.

Munich marathon

1 Vierschanzen-Tournee
www.vierschanzentournee.com
The best-known ski jump tournament in the world, held over New Year in Oberstdorf, Garmisch-Partenkirchen, Innsbruck and Bischofshofen.

2 FC Bayern Munich
www.fcb.de
Germany's world-famous football club has been picking up medals for years.

3 TSV 1860 Munich
www.tsv1860.de
Fans of the city's second football club refer to the team as "the Lions".

4 BMW Open
www.bmwopen.de
This tennis tournament (Apr/May) is held at the MTTC iphitos club.

5 BMW International Open
www.bmw-golfsport.com
The annual golf tournament (June) often takes place around Munich.

6 Munich Mash
www.munich-mash.com
See the pros in action (early July) performing stunts at Olympiapark.

7 Isarschwimmen
www.isarschwimmen.de
This traditional swimming event (first day of the Oktoberfest) sees brave individuals take to the Isar canal.

8 Munich Marathon
www.muenchenmarathon.de
Annual race (October) through the city.

9 Harness Racing
www.daglfing.de
Held throughout the year at the racecourse in Munich Daglfing.

10 Winter Running
www.olympiapark.de
A series of races in Olympiapark (Dec–Feb) on three courses (10, 15 & 20 km).

🔟 Munich for Free

1 Surfers on the Eisbach

The crowds of spectators on the bridge next to the Haus der Kunst can usually be seen from afar. What they've come to see is the surfers who ride the waves of the Eisbach rapids all year round (see p22).

Surfers on the Eisbach rapids

2 Gasteig

This cultural centre in Haidhausen offers free concerts, exhibitions, readings and courses almost daily, including concerts by the students at the Hochschule für Musik und Theater (see p112).

3 BMW Welt

The dynamic architecture of this futuristic building with its striking double cone entrance makes it well worth a visit. Exhibitions are free to enter (see p129).

The double cone at BMW Welt

4 Glockenspiel

The famous Glockenspiel chiming clock in the alcoves of the Neues Rathaus springs into action every day at 11am and noon (and again at 5pm in summer). The top section depicts the wedding of Duke Wilhelm V and Renate von Lothringen with a jousting tournament. Beneath them is the coopers' dance (see p12).

5 Museums and Galleries

The Museum für Abgüsse Klassischer Bildwerke (Katharina-von-Bora-Straße 10), Geologisches Museum (Luisenstraße 37), Kartoffelmuseum (Grafinger Straße 2), Feuerwehrmuseum (An der Hauptfeuerwache 8) and Lothringer 13 (see p43) all offer free admission. A number of other major museums (including the Pinakotheken) are also free for under-18s.

6 Olympiapark

While many of the attractions at Olympiapark have an entry fee, it doesn't cost a thing to wander the site, admiring the 1970s architecture of various Olympic venues. For fans of fireworks, the Sommernachtstraum (Midsummer Night's Dream) event in July puts on a spectacular display. You can even pack up a picnic and listen from inside the park whenever major concerts take place at the stadium (see pp32–3).

Free concert at Theatron

7 Theatron
At Whitsuntide and for three weeks in the summer, free concerts are held at the amphitheatre in Olympiapark (see p75).

8 Training at FC Bayern
www.fcbayern.com/shop
Experience a training session with the masters: fans can visit the stadium on Säbener Straße 51 to get up close and personal with their football heroes and maybe even bag an autograph. Dates of public training sessions are available on the club shop's website.

9 Open-Air Performances
www.mstheater.de
The Gärtnerplatztheater orchestra plays a free concert at the Gärtnerplatzfest in July. In summer and autumn, the Mohr-Villa and the amphitheatre on the north side of the Englischer Garten stage classic plays (see website for details). "Oper für alle" puts on a live transmission of an opera performance on Max-Joseph-Platz and a free festival concert on Marstallplatz in July.

10 Observatory at the Deutsches Museum
Excellent free tours of the observatory at the Deutsches Museum are available every Tuesday and Friday evening (see pp26–7).

MUNICH ON A BUDGET

1 MVV Group Tickets
The MVV (Munich's public transport network) offers cheap group tickets for up to five adults (children count as half an adult).

2 CityTourCard
For regular users of public transport, the CityTourCard also offers discounts on over 60 attractions (see 141).

3 Sightseeing by Tram
Take the scenic route: Tram 19 passes by Lenbachplatz, along Maximilan-straße, and across the Isar to Haidhausen – all for the price of a regular tram ticket.

4 Discovering the City on a Bike
MVG Rad is the name of the city's cycle-hire system – a great, inexpensive way to discover Munich (see p141).

5 Museums for a Euro
The state museums, along with some others, offer entry to the permanent exhibitions for just €1 on Sundays.

6 Sunset on the Terrace
You don't have to head to a pricey rooftop bar: the roof terrace of the café at Vorhoelzer Forum has a great view and reasonably priced drinks (see p101).

7 Fine Dining on a Shoestring
Many gourmet restaurants – even some with Michelin stars – have extremely reasonable lunch menus.

8 District Festivals
These events usually offer free entertainment and cheap food.

9 Picnic in the Beer Garden
You can take your own snacks to any beer garden and just pay for drinks.

10 Kinotag
For cut-price movie tickets, Kinotag (cinema day) is on Mondays (also Tuesdays in some cinemas).

Kinotag at the City Kinos

🔟 Festivals and Open-Air Events

1 Dance
Every 2 years in May (2019, 2021) ▪ www.dance-muenchen.de

This innovative dance festival takes place at about ten different venues around the city, including the Gasteig and Residenztheater.

Streetlife Festival

2 Streetlife Festival
May/Jun & Sep ▪ www.streetlife-festival.de

This sustainability festival organized by Green City takes place along Leopoldstraße and Ludwigstraße over two weekends a year. The Corso Leopold street festival is held at the same time.

3 Münchener Biennale
Every 2 years in May/June (2018, 2020) ▪ (089) 2805607
▪ www.muenchenerbiennale.de

The first of its kind in the world, this musical theatre festival was founded in 1988 by composer Hans Werner Henze (1926–2012). The city of Munich commissions young composers to write their first full work for the festival. Now a biennial event, the festival has become an established fixture with a diverse programme.

4 Filmfest
Smaller than the Berlin festival and not quite as star-studded, this film festival has made a name for itself as a festival of the people (see p54).

5 Opernfestspiele
End June–end July
▪ www.bayerische.staatsoper.de

Under Ludwig II, Munich grew into a centre of music, and it was the site of premieres of Wagner's operas and of a major Mozart festival. In 1910, the Richard Strauss festival week was launched, a tradition continued in the Opernfestspiele (Munich Opera Festival), which features both classic works and contemporary pieces. There are also free "Opera for all" performances held.

6 Tollwood
Summer festival (Jun/Jul) in Olympiapark South, winter festival (Nov–New Year) at Theresienwiese
▪ (0700) 3838 5024 (tickets)
▪ www.tollwood.de

A twice-yearly music, dance and theatre festival, held in both summer and winter. Formerly an alternative event, it has matured into a major festival with a wide-ranging programme of performances, vendors and organic foods.

Tollwood Festival at night

7 Königsplatz Open Air

Jul–Aug ▪ www.kinoopenair.de

The pompous backdrop of the Königsplatz seems tailor-made for open-air events. In summer, you can enjoy a wide variety of concerts here, from classical to rock and pop. The large square is also used for open-air film screenings.

8 Theatron Musiksommer and PfingstFestival

Whitsun, Aug ▪ www.theatron.de

At Whitsuntide as well as for 24 days during the summer, the amphitheatre at Olympiapark hosts a variety of musical events. The programme features artists from around the globe, and there's a real laid-back vibe about the whole event.

The Oktoberfest

9 Oktoberfest

The largest beer festival in the world *(see pp34–5)* runs in Munich for 16 or 17 days, ending on the first Sunday in October.

10 SpielArt

Every 2 years in Oct & Nov (2019, 2021) ▪ www.spielart.org

Munich's "window on the world of theatre" presents new productions from around the world at various venues, usually with a focus on one country.

OTHER EVENTS

Performers at BallettFestwoche

1 BallettFestwoche
Apr ▪ www.bayerische.staatsoper.de
In-house productions by the Staatsballett with guest performances.

2 Frühlingsfest
Mid-Apr–start of May
The Oktoberfest's little sister, held on the Theresienwiese.

3 DOK.fest München
International documentary films, premieres and work from up-and-coming directors *(see p 55)*.

4 Stadtgründungsfest
Weekend closest to 2 June
A cultural programme between Marienplatz and Odeonsplatz.

5 Brunnenhofkonzerte
Jun–Aug ▪ www.muenchen.de
Enjoy classical music, tango, movie scores and many other genres at the Residenz on warm summer nights.

6 Krimifestival
Spring and autumn ▪ www.krimifestival-muenchen.de
International crime thriller authors visit the Isar to perform readings.

7 Christopher Street Day
July ▪ www.csdmuenchen.de
Parade and show programme put on by the gay community.

8 Fantasy Filmfest
Horror films, thrillers and more *(see p55)*.

9 Stadtteilwochen
Summer, individual districts
Each district puts on its own week-long festival with food and cultural events.

10 Lange Nächte
www.muenchner.de
The "long night" of music is in May; the equivalent for museums is in Oct.

Munich Area by Area

Central Munich

🔟 Southern Old Town

Three of Munich's original city gates still stand, marking the boundaries of the southern old town: the Karlstor on Stachus, Sendlinger Tor and Isartor. Right at the centre of the old town is Marienplatz, Munich's main square. A former grain and salt market, it is now a key transport hub and a popular meeting place for locals. This part of the old town is also home to most of the city's shopping areas and pedestrian zones, as well as the Viktualienmarkt. Some of the oldest buildings in the city can be found in this part of Munich.

Virgin and Child, Mariensäule

Main altar of the Peterskirche

1 Peterskirche
MAP N4 ▪ Rindermarkt 1
▪ Tower: 9am–6:30pm Mon–Fri, 10am–7pm Sat and Sun (until 6pm in winter) ▪ Adm

The oldest church in the city dates back to the 12th century, although it has undergone a number of stylistic renovations since. A gilded figure of

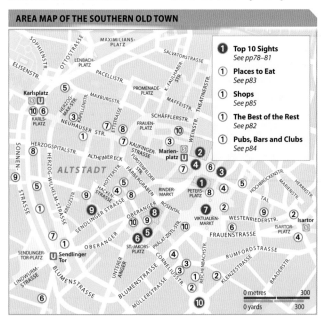

AREA MAP OF THE SOUTHERN OLD TOWN

1 **Top 10 Sights**
See pp78–81

1 **Places to Eat**
See p83

1 **Shops**
See p85

1 **The Best of the Rest**
See p82

1 **Pubs, Bars and Clubs**
See p84

St Peter stands in the middle of the imposing main altar and the remains of St Munditia are on display in a glass coffin. The view from the 91-m (299-ft) high tower is spectacular.

2 Neues Rathaus
MAP N3

The magnificent Neo-Gothic New Town Hall was built by Georg Hauberrisser between 1867 and 1909 and is home to the mayor's office. Ninety-minute guided tours of the building run on three days a week – a lift takes visitors up to the 85-m (279-ft) high observation deck in the tower (see pp12–13). At the top of the tower sits the city's mascot, the Münchner Kindl (a young monk). The Rathaus draws a crowd at least twice a day when its Glockenspiel starts to chime (at 11am and noon, also at 5pm in summer).

3 Altes Rathaus
MAP N4

Construction of the Gothic Old Town Hall on Marienplatz started in 1470 under architect Jörg von Halspach. The building was the seat of the city council until 1874 and is still a popular venue for official events, its ceremonial hall has a reconstructed late Gothic barrel vault and is

Restored façade of the Altes Rathaus

adorned with coats of arms. Once the city administration had relocated to the Neues Rathaus, the ground floor was converted to create a drive-through and a separate pedestrian passage on to Tal. The Altes Rathaus tower is now home to the toy museum (see p12).

4 Marienplatz
MAP N3–4

Munich's main square (see pp12–13) is dominated by the Neues Rathaus, while its eastern side is bounded by the Gothic Altes Rathaus. Both the Mariensäule and the Fischbrunnen are popular meeting spots, the latter dating back to the Middle Ages. Every year on Ash Wednesday, the fountain is the site of a traditional ceremony that started back in 1426: Geldbeutelwaschen, when the mayor and city councillors wash empty money bags for good luck. Marienplatz is a hive of activity, playing host to festivals, demonstrations, and FC Bayern celebrations (trophies are presented from the town hall balcony).

Vaulted ceiling in the Neues Rathaus

Synagoge Ohel Jakob (left) and the Jüdisches Museum München (right)

5 Synagoge Ohel Jakob
MAP M4 ■ St-Jakobs-Platz 18
■ (089) 20240 0100 (tours)

Munich's main synagogue, Ohel Jakob, was unveiled in November 2006. Its design, by architects Wandel Höfer Lorch, features two stacked cubes: a solid travertine base topped with a delicate glass structure and a metallic grid. The synagogue is the jewel in the crown of an ensemble comprising the Jewish Museum and a community centre. Access to the building is via an underground Corridor of Remembrance from the community centre.

6 Jüdisches Museum München
MAP M4 ■ St-Jakobs-Platz 16 ■ (089) 23 396096 ■ Open 10am–6pm Tue–Sun ■ Adm ■ www.juedisches-museum-muenchen.de

This freestanding cube of a museum with its wraparound glazing presents Jewish history and culture in Munich as part of its permanent exhibition, entitled "Stimmen – Orte – Zeiten" (Voices – Places – Times). It also puts on temporary exhibitions.

7 Viktualienmarkt
MAP N4 ■ Open 7am–8pm Mon–Sat

Viktualienmarkt exudes a unique atmosphere. This former farmers' market has become a real foodie destination, but it doesn't come cheap. The market has its own beer garden, as well as six fountains featuring local figures. Shrove Tuesday is always a great spectacle, when women come out from their stalls to take part in the famous "Tanz der Marktfrauen" (Dance of the Market Women). At the southernmost end of the market is Der Pschorr restaurant (see p83) and the reconstructed Schrannenhalle from 1853, which is home to the popular deli chain, Eataly.

8 Münchner Stadtmuseum
MAP M4 ■ St-Jakobs-Platz 1 ■ (089) 23 322370 ■ Open 10am–6pm Tue–Sun ■ Adm ■ www.muenchner-stadtmuseum.de

This museum occupies a number of buildings and documents the history and culture of the city across four permanent exhibitions. Some of the many highlights include the Morris Dancers sculpture by Erasmus Grasser, the special exhibit looking at Munich's role in the rise of the Nazis, and the film museum (see p54).

Costume (c.1840), Münchner Stadtmuseum

9 Asamkirche and Asam-Haus
MAP M4 ■ Sendlinger Straße 32–34 ■ Church open 8am–5:30pm daily

Between 1729 and 1733, Egid Quirin Asam purchased four separate properties on Sendlinger Straße. This is where he built his extensively stuccoed residence and – together with his brother Cosmas Damian – the Asamkirche (Church of St John of Nepomuk) of 1733. This late Baroque structure was intended to be a private church (it offered a direct view of the high altar from the Asam-Haus), but the city council refused to grant a construction permit until the brothers agreed to make it accessible to the public. Sandwiched between the houses, the church has no surface left unadorned. It overflows with cherubs and barley-sugar columns, false marble and stucco, frescos and oil paintings. The hidden windows of the interior let in only a little light, which evokes an almost mystical atmosphere (see p44).

Arial view of the Gärtnerplatz

⑩ Gärtnerplatz
MAP N4–5

This hexagonal square was laid out in 1860 and named to commemorate the German architect Friedrich von Gärtner. Its central fountain and flower beds lend it something of a Mediterranean feel. At the square's southern end is the Neo-Classical Staatstheater am Gärtnerplatz, a theatre dating from 1865 (see p53). The square now sits at the heart of the Gärtnerplatz quarter, renowned for its shops (see p69), restaurants and numerous cafés. The area is also home to Munich's gay and lesbian scene, along with the neighbouring Glockenbach quarter.

A DAY IN THE SOUTHERN OLD TOWN

▶ MORNING

Start the day with a coffee in **Cotidiano** (Gärtnerplatz 6) with a view of the **Staatstheater am Gärtnerplatz** and its namesake square. From here, take a stroll down the streets that lead away from Gärtnerplatz in a star shape and explore the many little shops and boutiques of the area. When you reach Rumfordstraße, take a left onto Utzschneiderstraße and you'll see the Schrannenhalle right ahead, which is now a branch of the Italian deli chain, **Eataly**. You can either buy a snack here or wait and check out the wide selection on offer at **Viktualienmarkt**. Here you can enjoy lunch in the beer garden, with a great view of the maypole in the middle of the square.

AFTERNOON

Once you've refuelled, head down Prälat-Zistl-Straße and turn right onto St-Jakobs-Platz to reach the boldly designed, modern synagogue, the **Jüdisches Museum** and the Münchner Stadtmuseum. Be sure to visit the "Typisch München" (Typical Munich) exhibit at the Stadt-museum. Next on the list is a walk down Oberanger, taking a right turn onto Schmidstraße towards **Sendlinger Straße**. This is where you will find the incredible piece of Baroque that is the **Asamkirche** and Asam-Haus. Now head north as far as **Marienplatz**, where the famous Glockenspiel attraction awaits you at the **Neues Rathaus** at 5pm (Mar–Oct). Try to find a spot for dinner in one of the busy restaurants along **Tal** or around the Viktualienmarkt.

See map on p78

The Best of the Rest

1 Sendlinger Tor
MAP M4

This city gate (Stadttor) from 1318 is overgrown with wild vines and marks the southern entrance to Sendlinger Straße.

2 Isartor
MAP N4 ▪ Tal 50 ▪ (089) 223266 ▪ Open 11am–5:30pm Mon, Tue & Thu–Sat, 10am–6pm Sun ▪ Adm ▪ www.valentin-musaeum.de

The Valentin-Karlstadt-Musäum in the south tower of the Isartor is devoted to cabaret artists Karl Valentin and Liesl Karlstadt. The Turmstüberl (museum café) is furnished in *fin-de-siècle* style.

3 Bürgersaalkirche
MAP M3 ▪ Neuhauser Straße 14

The Bürgersaal (community hall) has been used as a church by the Sodality of Our Lady since 1778.

4 Heiliggeistkirche
This Viktualienmarkt church is one of the oldest in the city (see p45).

Heiliggeistkirche on Viktualienmarkt

5 Künstlerhaus
MAP M3 ▪ Lenbachplatz 8

The Künstlerhaus (House of Artists) on Lenbachplatz was once a meeting place for artists and Munich society. It now hosts cultural events.

The Karlstor city gate

6 Karlstor and Stachus
MAP M3

Karlsplatz/Stachus, with its fountains and the medieval Karlstor, marks the end of the pedestrian zone.

7 Michaelskirche
This Jesuit church in the pedestrian zone is a prime example of Renaissance architecture (see p44).

8 Deutsches Jagd- und Fischereimuseum
MAP M3 ▪ Neuhauser Straße 2 ▪ (089) 220522 ▪ Open 9:30am–5pm daily ▪ Adm ▪ www.jagd-fischerei-museum.de

Hunting and fishing displays, including jackalope-type creations, in the former Augustinerkirche.

9 Bier- und Oktoberfestmuseum
MAP N4 ▪ Sterneckerstraße 2 ▪ (089) 24 231607 ▪ Open 1–6pm Tue–Sat ▪ Adm ▪ www.bier-und-oktoberfestmuseum.de

Housed in a medieval building, this museum presents Munich's history of beer along with everything you need to know about Oktoberfest.

10 Ignaz-Günther-Haus
MAP M4 ▪ St-Jakobs-Platz 20

This 16th-century late Gothic house was the home and studio of sculptor Ignaz Günther (1725–75).

Places to Eat

PRICE CATEGORIES
Price of a three-course meal (or similar)
for one with a glass of wine or beer,
including taxes and service.

€ below €30   €€ €30–60   €€€ over €60

1 Zum Augustiner
MAP M3 ▪ Neuhauser Straße 27
▪ (089) 2318 3257 ▪ €

A local Bavarian favourite with
mussel hall and arcaded garden.

2 Bratwurstherzl
MAP N4 ▪ Dreifaltigkeitsplatz 1
▪ (089) 295113 ▪ Closed Sun ▪ €

Bavarian classics such as *Saueres
Kalbslüngerl* (pickled veal's lung) or
Saure Zipfel (pickled sausage).

3 Nürnberger Bratwurst Glöckl am Dom
MAP M3 ▪ Frauenplatz 9
▪ (089) 291945 ▪ www.bratwurst-
gloeckl.de ▪ €

Among the dishes on offer here is
the famous *Rostbratwürste mit Kraut*
(barbecued sausages with cabbage).

4 Prinz Myshkin
MAP M4 ▪ Hackenstraße 2
▪ (089) 265596 ▪ €

Creative vegan and vegetarian
cuisine, served in an elegant setting
beneath high vaulted ceilings.

Minimalist interior at Prinz Myshkin

5 Schneider Bräuhaus
MAP N4 ▪ Tal 7 ▪ (089) 290
1380 ▪ www.schneider-brauhaus.de
▪ €

Munich flavours at their best: offal,
sausage and roast pork served with
cold Schneider Weisse beer.

Coffee shop Café Fräulein

6 Café Fräulein
MAP N4 ▪ Frauenstraße 11
▪ (089) 203 20710 ▪ €

A small coffee shop serving delicious
cakes and *Zimtschnecken* (cinnamon
rolls), as well as organic dishes.

7 Café Glockenspiel
MAP N3 ▪ Marienplatz 28
(entrance on Rosenstraße)
▪ (089) 264256 ▪ €€

Offering home-made cakes by day
and international cuisine at night.

8 Café Rischart
MAP N4 ▪ Viktualienmarkt 2
▪ (089) 231 700330 ▪ €

This café has a terrace with beautiful
views. Its flagship branch can be
found on Marienplatz.

9 Stadtcafé
MAP M4 ▪ St-Jakobs-Platz 1
▪ (089) 266949 ▪ €

A popular spot for museum visitors by
day. In the evening, it draws more of a
hipster crowd. Great beer garden.

10 Der Pschorr
MAP N4 ▪ Viktualienmarkt 15
▪ (089) 44238 3940 ▪ €€

From its restaurant, beer garden and
terrace, Der Pschorr offers Bavarian
cuisine and traditional beer culture.

See map on p78

Pubs, Bars and Clubs

Bar Dahoam at Milchbar

1 Milchbar
MAP M4 Sonnenstraße 27
■ (089) 4502 8818 ■ Open Mon–Thu
from 10pm, Fri & Sat from 11pm
■ www.milchundbar.de

Fans of house and electro flock here
for the excellent DJ sets. Start the
week off right with the regular Blue
Monday 1980s party.

2 Niederlassung
MAP N4 ■ Buttermelcherstraße
6 ■ (089) 3260 0307 ■ Closed Mon

This quaint, cosy pub has a excellent
gin selection (over 60 different types).
Happy hour for cocktails is from 7 to
9pm and again after midnight.

3 Paradiso Tanzbar
Red velvet, mirrors and crystal
chandeliers – these opulent
surroundings served as the
background for Freddie Mercury's
Living on My Own (see p56).

4 Buena Vista Bar
MAP N4 ■ Am Einlass 2a ■
(089) 2602 2811 ■ Closed Mon

A slice of Cuba in the heart of
Munich, with the image of Che
hanging proudly over the bar and
music by the Buena Vista Social
Club. Happy hour is from 6 to 8pm,
and there's a tapas menu.

5 Café Cord
MAP L4 ■ Sonnenstraße 19
■ (089) 54 540780 ■ Closed Sun

This retro-style café has a large,
attractive terrace. Food on offer
includes burgers (vegetarian options
available), sandwiches and salads.

6 Palau Grill & Drink
MAP M4 ■ Thalkirchner Straße
16 ■ 0152 5958 9137 ■ Closed Sun

It's always jam-packed at this
Catalan bar, with a thoroughly buzzy
atmosphere. Keep hunger at bay with
a selection of bocadillos and tapas.

7 Kennedy's Bar & Restaurant
MAP M4 ■ Sendlinger-Tor-Platz 11
■ (089) 5998 8460

A winning combination of restaurant
and Irish pub, this venue offers live
music and a beer garden.

8 Bohne & Malz
MAP M3 ■ Sonnenstraße 11
■ (089) 295202

This pub, which has outdoor seating,
serves breakfasts, Mediterranean-
style dishes and cocktails.

9 Cord Club
This club plays an eclectic mix
of music and holds an open mic
night on Fridays *(see p57)*.

10 Kilians Irish Pub
MAP N3 ■ Frauenplatz 11
■ (089) 2421 9899

Irish pub, complete with Irish stew
on the menu, Guinness, and live
music. Karaoke every Sunday.

Outdoor tables at Kilians Irish Pub

Shops

1 Kauf Dich Glücklich
MAP N4 ■ Reichenbach-straße 14

One of two branches in Munich offering the latest trends from niche clothes designers to well-known brands. Also sells a selection of shoes, music and gifts.

2 Blutsgeschwister
MAP N4 ■ Gärtnerplatz 6

Each branch of this chain has its own unique name, with this flagship outlet in Munich known as "German Schickeria". Occupying a prime position on Gärtnerplatz, it sells a range of women's clothing and accessories.

Blutsgeschwister's "German Schickeria" branch

3 CHI*KA so kind
MAP N4 ■ Müllerstraße 1

This store is brimming with lovingly selected items for children, including organic children's and baby clothes from boutique design workshops, innovative and educational toys, and much more.

4 Globetrotter
MAP N4 ■ Isartorplatz 8–10

Lovers of the great outdoors need look no further: everything you could possibly want or need is right here, along with a canoe testing pool, cold room, a climbing wall and a children's play area.

Hofstatt arcade

5 Hofstatt
MAP M4 ■ Sendlinger Straße 10

Once the home of the *Süddeutsche Zeitung* newspaper, this shopping mall has its own inner courtyards and sells fashion, accessories, cosmetics and food.

6 Ludwig Beck
MAP N3 ■ Marienplatz 11

Otherwise known as "Store of the Senses", this shop is in a league of its own for fashion, lingerie, stationery and music.

7 Kaufingerstraße and Neuhauser Straße
MAP M3

This pedestrian zone is Munich's biggest shopping street *(see p68)*.

8 Sendlinger Straße
MAP M4

This traditional shopping street is now home to the modern Hofstatt – a new shopping mall.

9 Servus Heimat
MAP M4 ■ Brunnstraße 3

Not your average souvenir shop, this place specializes in fun trinkets for Bayern fans.

10 Stachus-Passagen
MAP M3 ■ Karlsplatz

There are nearly 60 shops and eateries occupying the lower floor of the S-Bahn.

See map on p78 ←

🔟 Northern Old Town

In the northern part of the old town cluster some of Munich's most important sights. Extending north from Marienplatz as far as the top of the Altstadtring, this area includes the Frauenkirche and Theatinerkirche, as well as the Residenz palace complex and its Hofgarten. There are plenty of other sights too, including the long Promenadeplatz and its monuments, the Maximiliansplatz (one of the city's nightlife hubs), the Hotel Bayerischer Hof, and Odeonsplatz – once home to the Schwabinger Tor. This formed part of the second set of town ramparts, until the gate was torn down in 1817 to create the junction between Odeonsplatz and Ludwigstraße. In spite of all these attractions, it is a somewhat smaller square that is better known by far: Platzl, which is home to the world's most famous beer hall, the Hofbräuhaus.

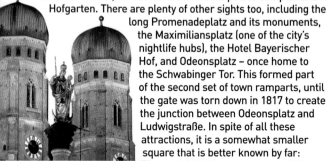

The towers of the Frauenkirche

AREA MAP OF THE NORTHERN OLD TOWN

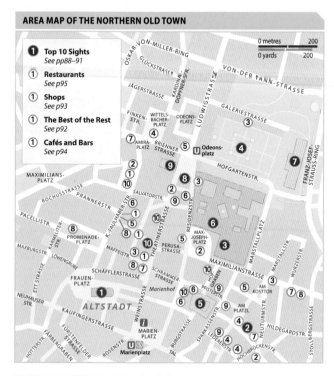

❶ **Top 10 Sights**
See pp88–91

① **Restaurants**
See p95

① **Shops**
See p93

① **The Best of the Rest**
See p92

① **Cafés and Bars**
See p94

① Frauenkirche
MAP M3

Visible from much of the city centre, the Frauenkirche's twin towers dominate the Munich skyline. The design for this enormous church originally included Gothic spires, but unfortunately there was not enough money left to build them. It was not until 36 years later that the Frauenkirche's domes were added, and these would effectively become the model for all subsequent Bavarian onion domes (see pp14–15).

② Platzl and Hofbräuhaus
MAP N3 ▪ Am Platzl 9 ▪ (089) 29013 6100 ▪ www.hofbraeuhaus.de

Munich and beer go back a long way: the Hofbräuhaus (1897) originated from a brewery (Hofbräu) founded by Wilhelm V in 1589. To this day, Hofbräu remains a Bavarian brand. The pub offers space for a thousand drinkers in its ground-floor bar, while the first floor is home to a ceremonial hall with a barrel vault ceiling, as well as a quieter bar. Outside the building itself, the Hofbräuhaus has an attractive beer garden sheltered by chestnut trees. It goes without saying that Hofbräu is served on tap – around 10,000 litres (21,134 US pints) a day, in fact. Away from the beer hall, the winding side streets that run off Platzl are the oldest part of Munich.

The Nationaltheater

③ Nationaltheater and Residenztheater
MAP N3 ▪ Max-Joseph-Platz 2 ▪ (089) 21 851920 ▪ www.staatsoper.de ▪ Max-Joseph-Platz 1 ▪ (089) 21 851940 ▪ www.residenztheater.de

The Nationaltheater has been the home of opera in Munich since it opened in 1818. It is also home to the state orchestra and ballet. The Opernfestspiele (opera festival) brings fans here from around the world every summer (see p74). Following the destruction of the Residenz-theater in World War II, a new building was constructed between the Residenz and Nationaltheater. It is home to the Bavarian State Theatre, which sets the standard for German-language productions (see p52).

Interior of the Hofbräuhaus, the world's most famous beer hall

The Temple of Diana in the Hofgarten

4 Hofgarten
MAP N2–3

Head through the Hofgarten archway on Odeonsplatz to reach the Renaissance garden, which was established while the Residenz was undergoing its extension work (see pp16–7).

5 Alter Hof
MAP N3 ■ Burgstraße 4 ■ Open 10am–6pm Mon–Sat

The Alter Hof is situated to the northeast of Marienhof (behind the Neues Rathaus) and is best reached via an archway among the old town houses on Burgstraße. The first Residenz of the Wittelsbachs within the city walls was built between 1253 and 1255. Original features include the west wing, which has its own gatehouse adorned with coats of arms, and a tower-like bay window known as the *Affenturm* (monkey's

tower). Legend has it that the court monkey kidnapped Ludwig IV (who would later become emperor of Germany), and climbed with him to the top of the turret. Fortunately, the boy was soon brought back safe and sound by the monkey. The vaulted cellar of the Alter Hof contains a permanent exhibition on Bavarian castles, which includes information on the former Residenz.

6 Residenz
MAP N3

Munich's must-see palace was built over the centuries as a city-centre residence for the Wittelsbach rulers of Bavaria, after they outgrew the Alter Hof (see pp16–17).

7 Staatskanzlei
MAP N2–3 ■ Franz-Josef-Strauß-Ring 1 ■ Tours Mon–Fri ■ reservations (089) 21 652450

The Bayerische Staatskanzlei (Bavarian State Chancellery; 1993), behind the Hofgarten, was the source of much controversy due to its ultra-modern design. Today, the complex combines the renovated cupola of the former army museum and a modern glass construction that was built over other historical structures.

8 Feldherrnhalle
MAP N3 ■ Odeonsplatz

Ludwig I commissioned Friedrich von Gärtner to build the Feldherrnhalle at the south end of Odeonsplatz, based on the Loggia dei Lanzi

Bayerische Staatskanzlei, the Bavarian State Chancellery

in Florence, and it was completed in 1844. The statues here represent the Bavarian Feldherren (generals), the Count of Tilly and Baron von Wrede. The entrance steps are guarded by two lions. The building is not open to the public and can only be viewed from the outside.

The Baroque-Rococo Theatinerkirche

⑨ Theatinerkirche
MAP N3 ▪ Theatinerstraße 22
▪ Open daily ▪ Fürstengruft crypt: May–Oct: 11:30am–3pm Mon–Sat ▪ www.theatinerkirche.de

Construction of the St Catejan court church, better known to locals as the Theatinerkirche, was begun in 1663 by Agostino Barelli. Enrico Zuccalli took over the project in 1674, and it was a good 100 years before François de Cuvilliés designed the Rococo façade. The crypt is the final resting place of the Wittelsbachs, including Emperor Karl VII (see p45).

⑩ Kunsthalle der Hypo-Kulturstiftung
MAP N3 ▪ Theatinerstraße 8 ▪ 10am–8pm daily (for exhibitions)

Built in 2001, the Kunsthalle buried deep within the glitzy Fünf Höfe shopping centre presents three to four high-profile exhibitions each year. Its themes range from Auguste Rodin and Walt Disney right through to the royal tombs of the Scythians.

A DAY IN THE NORTHERN OLD TOWN

▶ MORNING

This tour starts at the **Frauenkirche**. After exploring the cathedral, make your way around the building to Albertgasse. At the end of this alley, you will reach **Marienhof**, which you should cross to get straight to **Dallmayr**. After visiting the delicatessen, take a right and turn off Dienerstraße onto Hofgraben before turning right again onto Alter Hof. Take a left here onto Sparkassenstraße and just a few steps left again will get you to Münzstraße. The **Hofbräuhaus** at **Platzl** will be on your left. From here, head north past Platzl to Maximilianstraße. After taking in the small shops and boutiques on the way, you will pass the **Staatsoper** before arriving back at Theatinerstraße. **Aran Fünf Höfe** is a great place to stop for coffee and a snack.

AFTERNOON

Once you've enjoyed a pit stop, explore the **Fünf Höfe** shopping centre, or the Kunsthalle. Take the exit onto Kardinal-Faulhaber-Straße and turn right to reach the **Salvatorkirche** and **Literaturhaus**. Salvatorstraße then takes you back to Theatinerstraße once again. If you keep left, you will soon come to **Odeonsplatz**, where you will find the **Theatinerkirche** and **Feldherrnhalle**. Depending on the weather, you can spend the afternoon outside in the **Hofgarten** or at the **Residenz**. Once you've worked up an appetite, the **Spatenhaus an der Oper** is the perfect place to round off the day in style.

See map on p88

The Best of the Rest

Deckchairs outside the Literaturhaus

1 Literaturhaus
MAP N3 ■ Salvatorplatz 1
■ www.literaturhaus-muenchen.de

Located in a former Renaissance school, the Literaturhaus is used for literary gatherings and exhibitions. The OskarMaria brasserie can be found on the ground floor.

2 Max-Joseph-Platz
MAP N3

The Maximilian I Joseph memorial can be found in this early 19th-century square, which began with the construction of the Nationaltheater opera house. In summer, "Oper für alle" (Opera for all) streams the live performance on a giant screen.

3 Deutsches Theater-museum
MAP N2 ■ Galeriestraße 4a ■ 10am–4pm Tue–Sun ■ Adm

This museum and library in the Hofgarten arcades showcases the history of German theatre.

4 Wittelsbacher-platz
MAP N2

Wittelsbacherplatz, the square just to the west of Odeonsplatz, is home to Ludwig Ferdinand's palace (now the headquarters of Siemens) and an equestrian statue of Maximilian I.

5 Palais Porcia
MAP N3 ■ Kardinal-Faulhaber-Straße 12

The Rococo façade of this 1693 palace was designed by François de Cuvilliés the Elder.

6 Erzbischöfliches Palais
MAP N3 ■ Kardinal-Faulhaber-Straße 7

Formally the Palais Holnstein, the official residence of the archbishop is yet another creation of Cuvilliés the Elder, dating from 1737.

7 Münchner Kammerspiele

An Art Nouveau masterpiece, this theatre has an exciting programme of plays, music and dance (see p53).

8 Promenadeplatz
MAP M3

In medieval times, this long, narrow square with its five memorials served as a salt market. The famous Hotel Bayerischer Hof and the Palais Montgelas now occupy its northern side.

9 Alte Münze
MAP N3 ■ Hofgraben 4

The Münzhof (mint) lies to the northeast of the Alter Hof. Dating from 1567, its three-storey arcaded courtyard was once home to stables, a library and an art chamber belonging to Albrecht V. The official state mint was established here in the 19th century.

10 Salvatorkirche
MAP M3 ■ Salvatorstraße 17

Originally built in 1493–4, the Gothic cemetery church for the Frauenkirche has been a Greek Orthodox place of worship since 1829.

The Salvatorkirche

Shops

The *Sphere* at Fünf Höfe

1 Fünf Höfe
MAP N3 ■ www.fuenfhoefe.de

This elegant centre brimming with shops and restaurants attracts seven million visitors every year *(see p68)*.

2 Theatinerstraße and Residenzstraße
MAP N3

The shops on these streets mainly appeal to fashionistas with refined tastes *(see p68)*.

3 Maximilianstraße
MAP N3

Simply the most expensive shopping street in Munich *(see p68)*.

4 OBACHT'
MAP N4 ■ Ledererstraße 17

This shop on the corner of the Hofbräuhaus sells trinkets and curios with a local touch – perfect for souvenirs to take home.

5 Nymphenburger Porzellan
MAP N2 ■ Odeonsplatz 1

The flagship store of Porzellan Manufaktur Nymphenburg, located in the Nymphenburg rotunda, is popular with lovers of design and porcelain alike.

6 Manufactum
MAP N3 ■ Dienerstraße 12

A fitting venue for this warehouse of self-proclaimed "good things", Manufactum is located in the historical grounds of the Alter Hof, the first Residenz.

7 L'Occitane
MAP N3 ■ Maffeistraße 1

Experience the aromas of Provence and shop for luxury bath products, hand cream and fragrances at this branch of the global chain.

8 Elly Seidl
MAP N3 ■ Maffeistraße 1

Locals can't get enough of the handmade pralines sold by this family-run company.

9 Team shops: FC Bayern and TSV 1860 München
MAP N3 ■ Orlandostraße 1 and 8

Football kits and all kinds of team memorabilia can be found in these two shops, which are virtually opposite each other around the corner from the Hofbräuhaus.

Dallmayr's flagship store

10 Dallmayr
MAP N3 ■ Dienerstraße 14

The Marienhof branch of the former purveyor to the court has a top delicatessen and its own coffee blends. Its restaurant has two Michelin stars, and there's a lovely café bistro too.

See map on p88

Cafés and Bars

Stereo Café – a stylish hotspot

1 Café Kreutzkamm
MAP N3 ■ Maffeistraße 4

The home of the finest pralines and biscuits, this traditional café is the perfect spot in which to indulge.

2 Brasserie OskarMaria
MAP N3 ■ Maffeistraße 1

The café part of OskarMaria in the Literaturhaus serves its dishes on designer tableware (with quotes by Oskar Maria Graf). The gallery is a pretty spot, and outdoor seating is available in summer.

3 Schumann's Tagesbar
MAP N3 ■ Maffeistraße 6 ■ Closed Sun

This Fünf Höfe branch of the legendary Schumann's is a popular meeting place. Open during the day only.

4 Bar Centrale

A stylish Italian retro bar serving espressos in the morning and cocktails after sundown (see p62).

Fruity cocktail

5 Pusser's
MAP N3 ■ Falkenturmstraße 9

Pusser's is a classic piano bar with a menu of over 200 cocktails.

6 Stereo Café

This coffee shop on the sophisticated Residenzstraße is the perfect place to take a break during a busy day's shopping (see p63).

7 Café Luitpold
MAP N2 ■ Brienner Straße 11

Serving home-made pralines, cakes and daily specials, this former coffee house was rebuilt with its own palm garden after the war. It has a beautiful inner courtyard and fabulous conservatory.

8 Barista
MAP N3 ■ Kardinal-Faulhaber-Straße 11 ■ Closed Sun

Open from noon, this underground bar in Fünf Höfe shopping centre has a friendly atmosphere and upscale cuisine. It is also open in the evenings as a cocktail bar.

9 Café Maelu
MAP N3 ■ Theatinerstraße 32

From *macarons* to tarts, this coffee shop in the Theatiner arcade offers a selection of mouth-watering confections.

10 aran Fünf Höfe
MAP N3 ■ Theatinerstraße 12 ■ Closed Sun

This tiny café serves healthy bread, sweet treats and ice cream and what it lacks in space, it more than makes up with in flavour.

Restaurants

1 Pageou
■ €€€

The home of Ali Güngörmüş and his oriental-inspired cuisine (see p60).

2 Buffet Kull
MAP N4 ■ Marienstraße 4
■ (089) 221509 ■ €€

Innovative Mediterranean cuisine is on the menu at this restaurant with a bistro feel.

3 Pfälzer Residenz Weinstube
MAP N3 ■ Residenzstraße 1
■ (089) 225628 ■ €

The Residenz, comprising six lounges and a wine cellar, serves specialities such as *Saumagen* (sow's stomach), plus the best wines from the Palatinate region. Outdoor tables are available.

The world-famous Hofbräuhaus

4 Hofbräuhaus
■ €

Well known for its *Schweinshaxe* (ham hock) dishes, the Hofbräushaus also serves up some good vegetarian options (see p89).

5 Spatenhaus an der Oper
■ €€

Located opposite the opera house, this is the place to come for hearty, home-style cooking (see p66).

PRICE CATEGORIES
Price of a three-course meal (or similar) for one, with a glass of wine or beer, including taxes and service.

€ below €30   €€ €30–60   €€€ over €60

6 Restaurant Dallmayr
MAP N3 ■ Dienerstraße 14
■ (089) 213 5100 ■ Closed Sun & Mon
■ €€€

Chef Diethard Urbansky serves up spectacular six- and eight-course menus at this Michelin-starred restaurant on the first floor of the traditional delicatessen.

7 Matsuhisa Munich
■ €€€

The only restaurant in Germany headed up by top chef Nobu Matsuhisa serves exquisite Japanese fusion cuisine (see p61).

8 Kulisse Theater-Restaurant
MAP N3 ■ Maximilianstraße 26
■ (089) 294730 ■ € €€

For over 50 years, the Kulisse restaurant, café and bar at the Kammerspiele theatre have been serving fresh seasonal fare in a sophisticated atmosphere.

9 Restaurant Pfistermühle
MAP N3 ■ Pfisterstraße 4
■ (089) 2370 3865 ■ Closed Sun
■ €€–€€€

The vault of this 16th-century former ducal mill offers the finest in Bavarian cuisine. Lunchtime express menu available for €20.

10 KUFFLER Restaurant Bar Grill
MAP N3 ■ Hofgraben 9/Ecke Maximilianstraße ■ (089) 2422 4840
■ €€

Located in the former Residenzpost building with its beautiful dining room and wood-panelled Oak Room, this restaurant serves top-notch Mediterranean-influenced food.

See map on p88

🔟 Museum Quarter

The museum quarter (officially known as "Kunstareal München") is located in the Maxvorstadt district, bordering the university quarter. This is where you will find Bavaria's top art museums – the three Pinakotheken, Museum Brandhorst and the Egyptian Art Museum, among other world-class attractions.

The Glyptothek, Antikensammlungen and Lenbachhaus can also be found nearby, along with various smaller collections and a number of scientific museums, including the Paläontologisches Museum. With a selection of private galleries to boot, this area is definitely somewhere to spend a couple of days or more. There are plenty of cafés and bars where you can take a break in between museum visits. Alternatively, pack a picnic to enjoy in the parkland around the Pinakotheken.

Greek cup, Staatliche Antikensammlungen

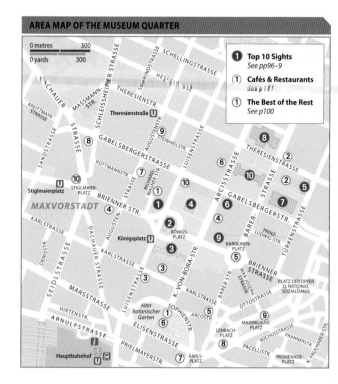

AREA MAP OF THE MUSEUM QUARTER

1. **Top 10 Sights**
   See pp96–9

1. **Cafés & Restaurants**
   See p101

1. **The Best of the Rest**
   See p100

MAXVORSTADT

Städtische Galerie im Lenbachhaus

1 Städtische Galerie im Lenbachhaus

MAP L2 ▪ Luisenstraße 33 ▪ (089) 23 332000 ▪ Open 10am–6pm Wed–Sun, to 8pm Tue ▪ Adm ▪ DA ▪ www. lenbachhaus.de

Franz von Lenbach's villa (1887–91) has its own living quarters, studio wing, a further wing extension and a historic garden. A shining brass cube was added during extensive renovations completed in 2013. Thanks to a world-first combination of daylight and LEDs, the famous Blue Rider collection and other works can be seen in a new light. Both the exhibition space on the U-Bahn mezzanine and Café Ella belong to the museum.

2 Königsplatz

MAP LM2

The city has Ludwig I to thank for this spacious square, with architect Leo von Klenze behind the Doric Propylaea and Ionian Glyptothek, which were built between 1816 and 1862. During the Nazi era, the square was paved and served as a parade ground. These days it is a green space and hosts outdoor events in the summer.

3 Staatliche Antikensammlungen

MAP LM2 ▪ Königsplatz 1 ▪ (089) 28 927502 ▪ 10am–5pm Tue–Sun (until 8pm Wed) ▪ Adm ▪ www.antike-am-koenigsplatz.mwn.de

This collection of antiquities includes Greek, Etruscan and Roman vases, and bronze, terracotta, glass and jewellery from the 3rd millennium BC to the 5th century AD.

4 Glyptothek

MAP M2 ▪ Königsplatz 3 ▪ (089) 28 927502 ▪ 10am–5pm Tue–Sun (until 8pm Thu) ▪ Adm ▪ www.antike-am-koenigsplatz.mwn.de

Munich's oldest public museum is the only one in the world that focuses exclusively on antique sculptures. Its highlights include 2,500-year-old archaic figures, the bust of Augustus, and the spectacularly lascivious Barberini Faun. The café is located in Room VIII and also offers seating out in the tranquil courtyard.

The Doric Propylaea in Königsplatz

The 21st-century multicoloured façade of Museum Brandhorst

5 Museum Brandhorst

MAP M2 ▪ Theresienstraße 35a
▪ (089) 23805 2286 ▪ 10am–6pm
Tue–Sun (until 8pm Thu) ▪ Adm ▪ DA
▪ www.museum-brandhorst.de

Opened in 2009, this museum occupies a purpose-built multi-coloured building by Berlin-based architects Sauerbruch Hutton. The polygonal area above the foyer was designed specially for Cy Twombly's famous *Lepanto Cycle*. Dominating some of the space are more of Twombly's large canvasses, while Andy Warhol is represented by some of his *Elvis* works, among others. Damien Hirst's work makes an appearance, as do artists including Jeff Koons, Sigmar Polke, Alex Katz and Bruce Nauman. The Horst Esskultur-Bar is situated in the foyer.

6 Staatliches Museum Ägyptischer Kunst

MAP M2 ▪ Gabelsbergerstraße 35
▪ (089) 2892 7630 ▪ 10am–8pm Tue,
10am–6pm Wed–Sun ▪ Adm ▪ DA ▪
www.smaek.de

The entrance to this museum on the site of the University of Television and Film Munich (HFF) is reminiscent of the entrance to a burial chamber in the Valley of the Kings, leading into underground halls around a sunken courtyard. The ramp to the exhibition space leads to a superb statue of the god Horus. Further highlights include a facial fragment of Akhenaten, the coffin mask of Queen Sitdjehutj, and a statue of High Priest Bakenkhonsu.

7 Pinakothek der Moderne

This enormous building was designed by Stephan Braunfels as a fitting temple to 20th- and 21st-century art and design. All of its rooms are grouped around a central rotunda. The café offers indoor and outdoor seating (*see pp18–21*).

8 Neue Pinakothek

The Neue Pinakothek (NP) opened in 1981 on the same site as its predecessor, which had been destroyed in World War II. Based on plans by Alexander von Branca, the new building offers exceptional lighting for its internal spaces, which are packed with world-class artworks. The Hunsinger restaurant here has outdoor tables on the terrace to enjoy on sunny days (*pp18–21*).

Van Gogh's *Sunflowers*, NP

⑨ NS-Dokumentations-zentrum

MAP M2 ▪ Brienner Straße 34 ▪ (089) 2336 7000 ▪ 10am–7pm Tue–Sun ▪ Adm ▪ DA ▪ www.ns-dokuzentrum-muenchen.de

A place of education and remembrance, this documentation centre presents Munich's past as the "Capital of the Movement". Opened in 2015, this cuboid structure of exposed white concrete stands on a historic spot: it was once the site of the "Brown House", the national headquarters of the Nazi Party. The permanent exhibition, "München und der Nationalsozialismus" (Munich and National Socialism), includes photographs, documents, texts, film projections and media stations.

NS-Dokumentationszentrum

⑩ Alte Pinakothek

This elongated building designed by Leo von Klenze has spacious rooms illuminated by skylights along with smaller cabinets on its north side, making it a model for other museum buildings of the early 19th century. The Alte Pinakothek suffered heavy damage in World War II, but it had been successfully rebuilt by 1957, with missing parts of the façade replaced by new, unrendered brickwork rather than reconstructed. The green spaces feature a sculpture exhibition, while the English-themed Café Klenze pays homage to the building's architects and is a good place for a break between museums (see pp18–19).

EXPLORING THE MUSEUM QUARTER

MORNING

A good breakfast at **Café Lotti** on Schleißheimer Straße will set you up for the museum tour. Head down Gabelsbergerstraße until you reach a right turn onto Richard-Wagner-Straße and you'll soon be at your first highlight – **Lenbachhaus**. Here, as with all of the following stops, you have the choice of stopping to browse the collections or moving on to the next museum. If you decide to keep going, turn left onto **Königsplatz**, where you'll find the **Glyptothek** and **Antikensamm-lungen**. Straight ahead takes you to the **NS-Dokumentations-zentrum**. Follow Brienner Straße until you reach Karolinenplatz and turn left onto Barer Straße to find yourself between the Alte Pinakothek (see below) and **Pinakothek der Moderne**. Make your way across the lawn in front of Pinakothek der Moderne and take in the colourful façade of **Museum Brandhorst**. Then, head around the museum building and treat yourself to an ice cream from **Ballabeni**. For something more substantial, keep going until you reach **Tresznjewski**.

AFTERNOON

Follow Theresienstraße, then turn left onto Barer Straße to reach the **Neue** or **Alte Pinakothek**. If you're interested in ancient Egypt, then take a left onto Arcisstraße and walk down to the **Staatliches Museum Ägyptischer Kunst**. From here, follow Arcisstraße across Katharina-von-Bora-Straße and see the day out at **Park Café**.

See map on p96

The Best of the Rest

Paläontologisches Museum

1 Paläontologisches Museum

MAP L2 ▪ Richard-Wagner-Straße 10 ▪ 8am–4pm Mon–Thu, 8am–2pm Fri

Visitors to the Palaeontology Museum can expect to find prehistoric fossils, including dinosaurs, mammoths, sabre-toothed tigers and the Mühldorf prehistoric elephant.

2 Museum Reich der Kristalle

MAP M1–2 ▪ Theresienstraße 41 ▪ 1–5pm Tue–Sun ▪ Adm

This museum next to the Pinakothek der Moderne holds a collection of minerals, crystals, precious stones, meteorites and much more.

3 Basilika St Bonifaz

MAP L2 ▪ Karlstraße 34

Dating back to 1850, this abbey is the final resting place of Ludwig I.

4 Hochschule für Musik und Theater

MAP M2 ▪ Arcisstraße 12

This university in the former "Führerbau" (Führer's building) is Germany's oldest training centre for music and theatre students. It also holds concerts.

5 Karolinenplatz

MAP M2

A black obelisk to commemorate those who fell in Napoleon's Russian Campaign of 1812 stands in this square, along with Amerikahaus and the stock exchange.

6 Alter Botanischer Garten

This former botanical garden is now a park (see p46).

7 Justizpalast

MAP L2 ▪ Prielmayerstraße 7

Built by Friedrich Thiersch in 1890–97, the Palace of Justice and its atrium dominate Karlsplatz/Stachus.

8 Lenbachplatz

MAP M3

This green square featuring the Wittelsbacherbrunnen, a classical fountain, is always busy with cars, trams and shoppers.

9 Maximiliansplatz

MAP M3

Some of Munich's most popular clubs are situated around this park-style square with its many memorials.

10 Löwenbräukeller

This historic building, dating back to 1883, has several rooms, a ceremonial hall and a large beer garden. The Triumphator barrel is tapped in March (see p67).

Löwenbräukeller – a traditional pub

Cafés and Restaurants

① Park Café
MAP L3 ▪ Sophienstraße 7 ▪ (089) 5161 7980 ▪ €€

This café occupies the site of the 1854 Glaspalast exhibition hall, before it burned down. Great beer garden.

Outdoor seating at Tresznjewski

② Tresznjewski
MAP M1 ▪ Theresienstraße 72 ▪ (089) 282349 ▪ €

Breakfast, lunch and dinner are served both inside and out at this café. In the evenings it transforms into a cocktail bar.

③ Hans im Glück
MAP L2 ▪ Luisenstraße 14 ▪ (089) 9993 7818 ▪ €

This burger paradise has something for everyone from beef lovers to vegans, and is great for satisfying post-pub hunger cravings.

Hans im Glück

④ Hamburgerei
MAP M2 ▪ Brienner Straße 49 ▪ (089) 2009 2015 ▪ €

The burgers at this joint are made with only the freshest ingredients. There are also crunchy salads and vegetarian and vegan options.

⑤ Hoiz
MAP M2 ▪ Karlstraße 10 ▪ (089) 2880 8809 ▪ Closed Sun ▪ €€

This cosy brasserie offers a small selection of high quality dishes at reasonable prices.

⑥ Café im Vorhoelzer Forum
MAP M1 ▪ Arcisstraße 21 ▪ €

This student café, with a panoramic terrace on the roof of the university, offers a great buffet brunch.

⑦ Vu Tang Kitchen
MAP L1 ▪ Augustenstraße 52 ▪ (089) 52350535 ▪ Closed lunch ▪ €€

This buzzy restaurant serves small plates of fresh and aromatic Laos fusion food.

⑧ Café Lotti
MAP L1 ▪ Schleißheimer Straße 13 ▪ (089) 6151 9197 ▪ €

This pink parlour-style café serves breakfast and light bites.

⑨ Café Jasmin
MAP L1 ▪ Steinheilstraße 20 ▪ (089) 4522 7406 ▪ €

Furniture from the 1950s, panoramic wallpaper and ruffled curtains set the scene for a range of (often organic) breakfast, lunch and cake options.

⑩ Café VON&ZU
MAP L2 ▪ Luisenstraße 22 ▪ (089) 21 930298 ▪ €

This café in the former Paul-Heyse-Villa offers wines (available in its own shop), snacks and seasonally inspired lunches.

See map on p96

🔟 Schwabing and the University Quarter

At the beginning of the 19th century, the expansion of the old town to the north and west of Odeonsplatz began with the development of Maxvorstadt, which is home to the university quarter, including Ludwig-Maximilians-Universität and parts of the Technische Universität. Neighbouring Schwabing was a separate village in its own right until it was incorporated into Munich in 1890, and became a well-known bohemian district, inhabited by artists and intellectuals. The Siegestor, a victory arch, is generally considered the entrance to Schwabing, although the "Schwabing vibe" extends as far as the fashionable Maxvorstadt quarter.

AREA MAP OF SCHWABING AND THE UNIVERSITY QUARTER

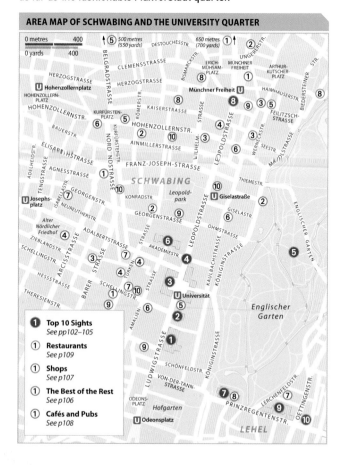

	Top 10 Sights	See pp102–105
	Restaurants	See p109
	Shops	See p107
	The Best of the Rest	See p106
	Cafés and Pubs	See p108

Siegestor, Munich's triumphal arch, at night

1 Bayerische Staatsbibliothek

MAP N2 ■ Ludwigstraße 16
■ www.bsb-muenchen.de

This major research library, which holds over 10 million books and 130,000 manuscripts, dates back to the 16th-century and incorporates the collections of Albrecht V and Wilhelm V. The present building was built by Friedrich von Gärtner in the style of a Renaissance palace.

2 Ludwigskirche

MAP N1 ■ Ludwigstraße 20

The Italian Romanesque-style university church, built between 1829 and 1843, is close to the Staatsbibliothek. King Ludwig I commissioned Friedrich von Gärtner to build the church that bears the monarch's name, on his monumental new boulevard, Ludwigstraße. The *Judgment Day* altar fresco by Peter Cornelius is the second-largest altar fresco in the world.

3 Ludwig-Maximilians-Universität

MAP N1 ■ Geschwister-Scholl-Platz
■ www.uni-muenchen.de

In 1826 Ludwig I moved the university founded in 1472 in Ingolstadt to Munich. Its main assembly hall looks out onto Geschwister-Scholl-Platz and is surrounded by faculty buildings.

4 Ludwigstraße and Siegestor

MAP N1

After the old town wall was pulled down in 1800, Ludwig I commissioned a monumental boulevard in Italian Renaissance style. This "Italian mile" is bounded by the Feldherrnhalle *(see pp90–91)* to the south and Siegestor to the north. Modelled on the Arch of Constantine in Rome, the Siegestor is crowned by the figure of Bavaria riding a chariot drawn by four lions. Designed for victory parades honouring the Bavarian army, the gate was inscribed after the war with lines that translate as "Dedicated to victory, destroyed in war, an entreaty for peace".

Ludwigskirche with its twin towers

Chinesischer Turm, Englischer Garten

⑤ Englischer Garten and Chinesischer Turm

Schwabing's "back garden" is a recreational paradise. The side streets on the right-hand side of Ludwigstraße and Leopoldstraße lead to two popular beer gardens: the Chinesischer Turm and Seehaus on Kleinhesseloher See (see pp22–3).

⑥ Akademie der Bildenden Künste

MAP N1 ▪ Akademiestraße 2–4 ▪ www.adbk.de

This elongated academy building built in Neo-Renaissance style between 1808 and 1886 has had an eventful history. The list of students who attended around 1900 reads like a who's who of modern art, including the likes of Kandinsky and Klee. An exhibition gallery is located on site.

⑦ Haus der Kunst

MAP P2 ▪ Prinzregentenstraße 1 ▪ (089) 2112 7113 ▪ 10am–8pm daily (until 10 Thu) ▪ Adm ▪ DA ▪ www.hausderkunst.de

The Nazi past of the "House of German Art", dating from 1937, is documented in a free exhibition in the entrance area. The Haus der Kunst is a non-collecting art museum that presents around eight international contemporary art exhibitions every year.

ART NOUVEAU

Munich is the birthplace of Jugendstil – the German version of Art Nouveau. In 1896, the first issue of the art journal *Jugend* (Youth) was published here, which gave the new movement – characterized by its decorative, floral and linear style – its name. As early as 1892, over 100 artists had joined forces against the "tyranny" of Franz von Lenbach to form the Munich Secession.

⑧ Leopoldstraße and Münchner Freiheit

MAP FG2–3

Passing beneath the Siegestor, you enter Schwabing and the district's principal promenade: Leopoldstraße. Flanked by shops, street-side cafés and fast-food outlets, the boulevard has lost some of its 1960s and 1970s atmosphere – the time when a new generation of film-makers, students and bohemians were setting the tone – but there are still some interesting pockets. One of the street's highlights is the *Walking Man* (1995), a 17-m (55-ft) high sculpture by Jonathan Borofsky in front of House No. 96. At the northern end of Münchner Freiheit, in a café of the same name, tables are set out in summer beneath a larger-than-life statue of actor Helmut Fischer, star of German TV series

Colonnade at the Haus der Kunst

Monaco Franze – Der ewige Stenz ("The Eternal Dandy"). Art-Nouveau houses can be found on side streets off Leopoldstraße, notably Georgenstraße (No. 8–10) and Ainmillerstraße (No. 20, 22, 33, 34, 35 and 37). Take a detour onto Kaisertraße for a glimpse of a pretty ensemble from the mid-19th century (Gründerzeit), or head to Hohenzollernstraße for a host of boutiques and shops. The other end of Leopoldstraße leads to the Englischer Garten.

Bayerisches Nationalmuseum

9 Bayerisches Nationalmuseum
MAP P2 ■ Prinzregentenstraße 3 ■ (089) 2112401 ■ 10am–5pm Tue–Sun (until 8pm Thu) ■ Adm ■ www.bayerisches-nationalmuseum.de

This museum, packed with exhibits spanning two millennia, offers a journey through the history of European art and culture. The building, dating from 1855, is almost as impressive as the exhibits, and worth the price of admission alone.

10 Sammlung Schack
MAP Q3 ■ Prinzregentenstraße 9 ■ 10am–6pm Wed–Sun ■ Adm

This collection features around 180 masterpieces of 19th-century German art, primarily landscapes and historical scenes, as well as legends and mythology.

A DAY IN THE UNIVERSITY QUARTER

MORNING

Begin your day at the **Café Münchner Freiheit**. Afterwards, stroll down Leopoldstraße and turn onto Kaiserstraße with its pretty houses (Lenin once lived at No. 46). Once you pass Kaiserplatz, follow Friedrichstraße to the corner of Ainmillerstraße with its Jugendstil houses (nos. 20–37). Continue along Friedrichstraße until you reach Georgenstraße. At no. 8 is the **Pacelli-Palais**, next door to the Palais Bissing. From here, return to Leopoldstraße and the **Akademie der Bildenden Künste** (Academy of Fine Arts) near the **Siegestor**. Walk to the university and cross the inner courtyard of the main building, which will bring you to the student district around Amalienstraße, with its many cafés and restaurants. If you're ready for a coffee break, give **Gartensalon** a try (Türkenstraße 90).

AFTERNOON

Once you've taken a break, it's time to head to the **Englischer Garten**. Amble along to the **Kleinhesseloher See** and take in the atmosphere. Make your way towards the beer garden at the **Chinesischer Turm** before climbing up to **Monopteros**, where the view of the city is simply magnificent. Next up, it's time to check out the surfers on the Eisbach and then explore an exhibition at the **Haus der Kunst**. See out the evening in style with a cocktail at **Die Goldene Bar** to the northeast.

See map on p102

The Best of the Rest

Interior of the Erlöserkirche

1 Elisabethplatz
MAP F3 ■ Market: Mon–Sat

A piece of old Schwabing, this square is named after the Austrian empress Sisi (short for Elisabeth). A market has been held here since 1903.

2 Erlöserkirche
MAP G2 ■ Germaniastraße 4

This Protestant Art Nouveau church (1899–1901) occupies the northern end of Münchner Freiheit.

3 Wedekindplatz
MAP G2

Renovated in 2014, this square was once the heart of rural Schwabing. In 1962, it was the site of the local riots, known as the "Schwabinger Krawalle" (see p41).

4 Alter Nordfriedhof
MAP F3 ■ Between Zieblandstraße, Arcisstraße, Adalbertstraße and Luisenstraße

There's nothing morbid about this former cemetery dating back to 1866. It is now a place of recreation and relaxation, and children love to play hide and seek amongst the old tombstones.

5 Luitpoldpark
MAP F1

This park was created out of rubble from World War II. The restaurant in Bamberger House features ornate guest rooms and a beautiful terrace.

6 Nikolaiplatz & Seidlvilla
MAP G3 ■ www.seidlvilla.de

The Seidlvilla on Nikolaiplatz was saved from demolition and is now a centre for culture and community.

7 Archäologische Staatssammlung
MAP P2 ■ Lerchenfeldstraße 2
■ Closed for renovation until 2020

A collection of ancient and prehistoric discoveries from Bavaria.

8 Kaiserplatz and Kaiserstraße
MAP F2

The silhouette of St Ursula's church on Kaiserplatz has been immortalised by Kandinsky. Kaiserstraße is flanked with ornate buildings from the Gründerzeit.

9 Palais Pacelli
MAP F3 ■ Georgenstraße 8

This listed palace is a Neo Baroque-style residential building.

Walking Man

10 Walking Man
MAP F3
■ Leopoldstraße 36

Jonathan Borofsky's dynamic 17 m (56 ft) sculpture was commissioned by the Munich Re insurance group.

Shops

1 Breitengrad
MAP N1 ■ Schellingstraße 29

This shop offers cups and mugs, jewellery, a limited selection of clothing, and bags, not to mention various useful (and useless!) goodies, such as gold sparklers.

2 Living Colour
MAP F2
■ Hohenzollernstraße 39

Clothes, pretty bags, cups, mugs, make-up bags and more – all featuring pretty, vibrant designs.

Quirky products at Living Colour

3 Apartment
MAP M1 ■ Barer Straße 49

Yet another shop offering all kinds of colourful products, including tableware, gifts, and countless whimsical bits and pieces for kids of all ages.

4 Lehmkuhl
MAP G2 ■ Leopoldstraße 45

This fine bookshop on Leopoldstraße was founded in 1903 before being taken over by Fritz Lehmkuhl in 1913. It has a distinguished inventory and holds regular author readings.

5 Kochhaus Schwabing
MAP F2
■ Hohenzollernstraße 74

The "accessible cookbook" is a new shopping concept created by this chain of grocery stores. It presents a variety of recipes to cook at home and groups all of the necessary ingredients together, so that customers can simply pick up everything they need at once. It also offers light bites and cooking courses.

6 Biervana
MAP F2
■ Hohenzollernstraße 61

Beer, ale and craft beer – this shop offers over 600 different types with a particular focus on craft beers. It also stocks speciality beers.

7 Picknweight
MAP N1 ■ Schellingstraße 24

Vintage by the kilo: this shop is brimming with second-hand clothes that you pay for by weight. Another branch can be found on Tal.

8 Autorenbuchhandlung
MAP F2 ■ Wilhelmstraße 41

As the name suggests ("Authors' Bookshop"), this bookshop was founded 40 years ago by authors who wanted to free themselves from the book industry. Many author readings are held here.

9 Welt White
MAP N2 ■ Theresienstraße 9

This store is a sparkling white wonderland of home accessories, stationery, ceramics, sweets and knick-knacks.

10 Dear Goods
MAP F3 ■ Friedrichstraße 28

This shop stocks only fair-trade, eco-friendly and vegan clothing, shoes and accessories.

Eco-friendly clothing at Dear Goods

See map on p102

Cafés and Pubs

1 Café Münchner Freiheit
MAP G2 ▪ Münchner Freiheit 20

This long-established multilevel café with a large outdoor seating area has a larger-than-life sculpture of German actor Helmut Fischer, which overlooks the tables.

Café Münchner Freiheit

2 Café Reitschule
MAP G3 ▪ Königinstraße 34

Located at the edge of the Englischer Garten, this traditional café boasts three patios, a beer garden and a conservatory. From the inside, patrons can see into the riding school. Champagne happy hour runs from 5 to 6:30pm.

3 Cotidiano
MAP F2 ▪ Hohenzollern- straße 11

The breakfast menu at this branch of Gärtnerplatz's cult café offers something for everyone, including delicious goods from the in-house bakery. It also serves light bites in the afternoon and evening. Outdoor tables are available.

4 Gartensalon
MAP N1 ▪ Türkenstraße 90 ▪ Closed Mon

Tucked away in an inner courtyard on the Amalienpassage, this café is colourful and kitsch, with rainbow furniture and photo-covered walls. The garden is also a floral paradise. Breakfasts here are particularly good. Cards not accepted.

5 Café an der Uni (Cadu)
MAP N1 ▪ Ludwigstraße 24

This delightful café on Ludwigstraße is the perfect place to stop for a coffee break while you're out and about in the university quarter.

6 Atzinger
MAP N1 ▪ Schellingstraße 9

This once-legendary student pub has been extensively modernized, but the prices remain reasonable.

7 Café Ignaz
MAP F3 ▪ Georgenstraße 67

This place has been serving delicious organic vegetarian and vegan goodies for over 30 years. It also has its own in-house bakery.

8 Die Goldene Bar
MAP P2 ▪ Prinzregentenstraße 1

Located within the Haus der Kunst, this bar takes its name from its golden walls. Enjoy light meals here in the afternoon or stay until evening for cocktails mixed by Klaus St Rainer, former bartender of the year. Outdoor seating is available.

9 Café Katzentempel
MAP N1 ▪ Türkenstraße 29

This vegetarian café is also home to six rescued cats, so you can enjoy a coffee with feline company.

10 Schall & Rauch
MAP N1 ▪ Schellingstraße 22

Small, cosy pub, serving local pasta dishes in a friendly atmosphere. Often packed to the rafters.

Exterior of the Schall & Rauch pub

Restaurants

Vivid dining room decor at Tantris

① Tantris
MAP G2 ■ Johann-Fichte-Straße 7 ■ (089) 3 619590 ■ noon–3pm, 6:30pm–1am Tue–Sat ■ €€€

This two-Michelin-starred restaurant is Munich's finest for haute cuisine.

② Georgenhof
MAP F3 ■ Friedrichstraße 1 ■ (089) 34 077691 ■ €€

An Art Nouveau-style restaurant with beer garden. Be sure to try the pork dishes *Schweinebraten* or *Schweinshaxe* (see p58).

③ Geisels Werneckhof
MAP G3 ■ Werneckstraße 5 ■ (089) 3887 9568 ■ 7pm–midnight Tue–Sat (also 1–4:30pm Sat) ■ €€€

A fine-dining experience inspired by Japanese cuisine. Five- and seven-course set menus only.

④ Ruff's Burger
MAP N1 ■ Türkenstraße 63 ■ €

Munich is in love with the burger and the tasty home-made ones here are made fresh every day. Also at Rindermarkt 6 and Occamstraße 4.

⑤ Occam Deli
MAP G2 ■ Feilitzschstraße 15 ■ €

Delicatessen with New York style snacks and light dishes.

⑥ Arabesk
MAP P2 ■ Kaulbachstraße 86 ■ (089) 333738 ■ Closed lunch on Sat & Sun ■ €€

Delicious Lebanese food. Customers have been enjoying the flavours of the Middle East followed by shisha here for over 30 years.

⑦ Max-Emanuel-Brauerei
MAP N1 ■ Adalbertstraße 33 ■ (089) 271 5158 ■ €

This traditional tavern dates back to around 1800 and serves traditional Bavarian dishes. Its annual white parties to celebrate Carnival, or Fasching, are legendary. Great beer garden with shaded areas.

⑧ Osterwaldgarten
MAP G2 ■ Keferstraße 12 ■ (089) 3840 5040 ■ €€

This idyllic beer garden and restaurant at the Englischer Garten serves Bavarian specialities. It is very popular so it is best to book ahead.

⑨ Riva Bar
MAP G2 ■ Feilitzschstraße 4 ■ (089) 30 905 1808 ■ €

This sister restaurant of the popular "Italia im Tal" also has a contemporary bar.

⑩ Anh-Thu
MAP F3 ■ Kurfürstenstraße 31 ■ (089) 2737 4117 ■ Open daily; closed Fri–Sun lunch ■ €€

This contemporary restaurant serves high-end Vietnamese cuisine.

See map on p102

🔟 Along the Isar

Four distinct neighbourhoods flank the right bank of the Isar river: Giesing, Au, Haidhausen and Bogenhausen. While Bogenhausen is studded with villas, Haidhausen – the "French quarter" – is a hotspot for nightlife. To the west of the Isar, on the left bank, lie the Englischer Garten and Lehel, a highly sought-after residential area containing some beautiful historic buildings. Most of the city's sights and attractions are located to the east of the river, including the Jugendstil masterpiece of the Müller'sches Volksbad, the Maximilianeum and Villa Stuck. Of the two islands in the middle of the Isar, Museuminsel holds the Deutsches Museum, a definite highlight in this area.

Friedensengel

AREA MAP OF ALONG THE ISAR

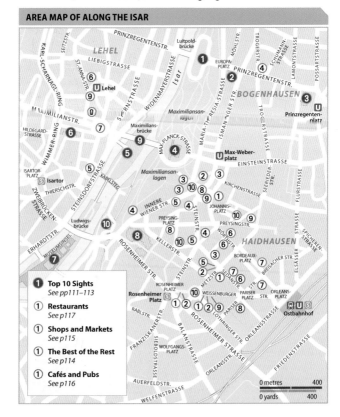

1 Top 10 Sights
See pp111–113

1 Restaurants
See p117

1 Shops and Markets
See p115

1 The Best of the Rest
See p114

1 Cafés and Pubs
See p116

0 metres   400
0 yards   400

Arches, columns and mosaics adorn the façade of the Maximilianeum

1 Friedensengel
MAP Q3 ■ Prinzregentenstraße

Soaring high above the banks of the Isar, the Friedensengel (Angel of Peace) of 1896–99 commemorates the Franco–Prussian war of 1870–71. Based on the Greek goddess Nike, this gilded figure stands 6 m (19.7 ft) tall. From its base, two sweeping flights of stairs lead down an escarpment to a terraced park with fountains.

2 Museum Villa Stuck
MAP Q3 ■ Prinzregentenstraße 60 ■ (089) 4 555510 ■ 11am–6pm Tue–Sun (until 10pm first Fri of month) ■ Adm ■ DA ■ www.villastuck.de

Not far from the Friedensengel is the Villa Stuck – the *fin-de-siècle* masterpiece of painter Franz von Stuck. A miller's son, Stuck quickly rose to fame and was instrumental in the creation of the Munich Secession in 1892, which "discovered" Jugendstil (the local version of Art Nouveau). The villa has served as a museum since 1968. On view are private rooms, a permanent Art Nouveau collection, and changing exhibitions in the studio wing.

3 Prinzregententheater
MAP R3 ■ Prinzregentenplatz 12 ■ www.theaterakademie.de

This theatre is one of several monumental buildings on this stretch of Prinzregentenstraße (see p52). The Bayerische Staatstheater

perform here, along with other companies. It was headed up by August Everding, whose legacy to the city includes the Bayerische Theaterakademie, a training ground for young talent. Next door is Prinzregentenbad, a public bath, and gourmet food shop Feinkost Käfer (see p115), is just across the street.

4 Maximilianeum
MAP Q4 ■ Max-Planck-Straße 1

Built by Friedrich Bürklein high on the banks of the river Isar, the Maximilianeum stands at the end of Maximilianstraße. Maximilian II commissioned this massive structure as a school for gifted students from poor backgrounds. Though the building has been the home of the Bavarian parliament since 1949, a school still occupies its rear; nowadays it accepts students with the highest grades.

The Prinzregententheater

5 Praterinsel and Alpines Museum

MAP P4 ■ Praterinsel 5 ■ (089) 2112240 ■ 10am–6pm Tue–Sun ■ Adm ■ www.alpenverein.de

The Alpines Museum, at the southern end of the Praterinsel, an island in the Isar, documents the history of mountaineering and features special exhibitions throughout the year. An educational garden displays the various types of rock found in alpine regions, while exhibitions and events are held in the halls of the former Riemer-schmid distillery located at the northern end of the island. Tango dancers gather in the courtyard on summer evenings.

6 Museum Fünf Kontinente

MAP P3 ■ Maximilianstraße 42 ■ (089) 21013 6100 ■ 9:30am–5:30pm Tue–Sun ■ Adm (free for under-18s) ■ www.museum-fuenf-kontinente.de

This impressive Neo-Renaissance building dates back to 1859–65 and was originally conceived for the Bayerisches Nationalmuseum. The ethnological museum made this its home in 1926 and it boasts over 160,000 exhibits on the culture of non-European nations, with a collection on Bavarian rulers dating back more than 500 years. The museum café, max2, serves food in the arcades of Maximilanstraße.

Kachina, Museum Fünf Kontinente

Transport at the Deutsches Museum

7 Deutsches Museum

Directly southwest from the Müller'sches Volksbad is the Deutsches Museum, the largest museum of science and technology in the world (see pp26–9).

8 Gasteig

MAP PQ5 ■ Rosenheimer Straße 5 ■ www.gasteig.de

The site of the former Bürgerspital hospital and Bürgerbräukeller was transformed into the Gasteig cultural centre between 1978 and 1985, and its tiled bunker design was controversial. The name comes from a portmanteau of the German for "quick climb, steep path". It is home to the Munich Philharmonic, the Carl-Orff concert hall and the state library.

9 The Isar Bridges

MAP P5–Q4

The Maximiliansbrücke is actually made up of two distinct bridges: the outer bridge leads to the Maximilianeum, while the inner bridge connects the west bank of

Gasteig, home to the Munich Philharmonic

HAIDHAUSEN

This area used to lie beyond the city boundaries. A poor, rural village, it was referred to as a Glasscherbenviertel or "broken glass district", and some of the renovated inns are still reminiscent of this period. After 1871, French reparation payments launched development in this area, which explains the French names of the streets here.

the Isar with the Praterinsel. Ludwigsbrücke is another historically important bridge. Henry the Lion ordered that the original Isarbrücke (built in 1157–58 by the Bishop of Freising) be demolished to make way for a new bridge further to the south, which is where the Ludwigsbrücke is located today. All of the Isar bridges offer lovely views up and down the slow-moving river.

An idyllic spot on the Isar:
Müller'sches Volksbad

⑩ Müller'sches Volksbad
MAP P4 ■ Rosenheimer Straße 1 ■ 7:30am–11pm daily ■ Adm ■ www.swm.de

Named for Karl Müller, the Munich citizen who financed the project, this Jugendstil bathing temple was built in 1897–1901, based on a design by Carl Hocheder. It was the first public pool in the city and remains one of the most beautiful. It is worth going for a swim just to admire the interior or enjoy the facilities, which include a steam room, though you can visit its stylish café without going for a dip.

A DAY ON THE ISAR

▶ MORNING

Setting off from **Müller'sches Volksbad** after coffee or breakfast at the in-house café, turn left out of the baths along the Isar to the footbridge, which leads to Prater-insel. Walk through the garden of the **Alpines Museum** and then across the island to Maximilians-brücke, which will take you directly to the **Maximilianeum**. Make your way past the building in a semicircle and turn right onto Sckellstraße, which leads to Wiener Platz, with its market stalls and the Hofbräukeller. The narrow lane called An der Kreppe runs from this square to several of the historic inns in the "Glasscherbenviertel". The beer garden at the **Hofbräukeller** is a great place to stop for a break.

AFTERNOON

After lunch, return to Sckell-straße, cross Max-Planck-Straße and head along Maria-Theresia-Straße, which is flanked by beautiful houses from the mid-19th-century/Jugendstil period. On the left-hand side of the street, the Maximiliansanlagen is a perfect park for a spot of ambling. Regardless of the route you take, all paths will eventually lead you to the **Friedensengel**. Continue along for just a couple of minutes until you reach **Villa Stuck**, the Jugendstil museum. After a tour of the museum, make your way to **Feinkost Käfer** on Prinzregentenstraße, a treat whether you opt for the deli bistro or the Käfer-Schänke fine-dining restaurant.

See map on p110 ←

The Best of the Rest

Johanniskirche's striking tower

⑥ Pfarrkirche St Anna
A Neo-Romanesque parish church, St Anna is the result of an architecture competition *(see p45)*.

⑦ Maxmonument and Upper Maximilianstraße
MAP P3

The stretch of Maximilianstraße from the Altstadtring is flanked by ornate public buildings. A monument to Maximilian II (the Maxmonument) stands at the centre of a roundabout.

⑧ Regierung von Oberbayern
MAP P3 ▪ Maximilianstraße 39

Maximilian II commissioned this Neo-Gothic building, which today serves as the seat of government for Upper Bavaria.

① Johanniskirche
MAP Q4 ▪ Johannisplatz

This Neo-Gothic church has a truly striking 90-m- (295-ft-) high tower.

② An der Kreppe
MAP Q4

Restored inns, originally designed for brick workers, give this corner of Haidhausen a village-like character.

③ Wiener Platz and Hofbräukeller
MAP Q4

At the heart of Haidhausen, Wiener Platz has hosted a market since 1889, while the Hofbräukeller has been here since 1892 *(see p64)*.

④ Nikolaikirche
MAP P4 ▪ Innere Wiener Straße 1

This small church, first recorded in 1313, is set on the river bank. Its cloister is modelled after the one at Altötting, a town east of Munich.

⑤ St Lukas
MAP P4 ▪ Mariannenplatz 3

St Luke's, in Lehel, built in 1893–96, is renowned for its choral concerts.

⑨ Lehel
MAP P3–4

Lehel is widely considered to be one of the city's most beautiful districts. A stroll in the area, especially in the vicinity of the Maxmonument, takes you past some stunning architecture.

⑩ Weißenburger Platz
MAP Q5

This square, with the Glaspalast-brunnen, a tiered fountain, at its centre, is the hub of the French quarter. An atmospheric Christmas market is held here every December.

The fountain in Weißenburger Platz

Shops and Markets

(1) Ypnotic
MAP Q5 ■ Weißenburger Str. 12

A new scarf in a great colour? Or maybe a jumper with an unusual design? Ypnotic stocks on-trend clothing by designers including Daily's, Freequent, Malvin and Anonyme, as well as a range of accessories.

(2) Weltladen München
MAP Q5 ■ Weißenburger Straße 14

From organic coffee to handmade paper from India, this shop stocks all sorts of fair trade products from around the world.

Livingroom shop and café

(3) Livingroom
MAP Q4 ■ Wiener Platz 2

Vintage furniture and accessories for the kitchen, bathroom and living room. There is also a café.

(4) Feinkost Käfer
MAP R3 ■ Prinzregentenstraße 73

Catering king Gerd Käfer's Bogenhausen delicatessen is the place where celebrities do their food shopping.

(5) Doppler Shop
MAP Q5 ■ Metzstraße 15 (entrance on Sedanstraße)

This is the place for quirky and unique homeware, from stationery through to tableware and cushions.

Cushion at the Doppler Shop

Cute trinkets on sale in Kokolores

(6) Kokolores
MAP Q5 ■ Wörthstraße 8

A shop full of interesting finds, from novelty postcards and stationery through to extra-special gifts.

(7) Hubercraft
MAP Q5 ■ Sedanstraße 23

Unusual and very colourful fashion, home accessories, decorations and knick-knacks.

(8) Mohrmann Basics
MAP Q4 ■ Innere Wiener Straße 50

Striking fashion that's anything but ordinary – this small shop attracts customers to Haidhausen from miles around. Mohrmann stocks a wide range of different labels.

(9) Buch & Töne
MAP Q5 ■ Weißenburger Str. 14

A charming bookshop stocking a mix of new and second-hand books, along with with audio-books and a selection of CDs.

(10) Markt am Wiener Platz
MAP Q4

The permanent market stalls at Wiener Platz are open on weekdays and sell exquisite foodstuffs, from Alpine cheeses to Greek olives. It's a lovely place to stop for a coffee too.

See map on p110

Cafés and Pubs

 Fortuna Cafebar
MAP Q5 ▪ Metzstraße 10

This small neighbourhood café with an Italian feel has tables both inside and out. It's an excellent place to come for Sunday brunch, and the hot chocolate is to die for.

KaffeeKüche's front terrace

 KaffeeKüche
MAP Q5 ▪ Weißenburger Straße 6 ▪ Closed Mon

The tables at this funky café can all be found outside in the small pedestrian zone. Tasty breakfast and mostly organic food.

 Negroni
MAP Q5 ▪ Sedanstraße 9 ▪ Closed Sun

Great cocktails are the order of the day at this American-style bar. The unpretentious menu features Italian-inspired cuisine.

 Barroom
MAP Q5 ▪ Milchstraße 17 ▪ Closed Sun & Mon

The smallest cocktail bar in Munich, this venue specializes in rum-based concoctions. Expect it to be busy.

Maria Passagne
MAP Q5 ▪ Steinstraße 42 ▪ (089) 486167 ▪ Closed Sun

The "living room" bar in this sushi restaurant is small and cosy. Booking is recommended, as the doorman stops letting anyone in once it's full.

PRICE CATEGORIES

Price of a three-course meal (or similar) for one, with a glass of wine or beer, including taxes and service.

€ below €30   €€ €30–60   €€€ over €60

 Café im Hinterhof
MAP Q5 ▪ Sedanstraße 29

This Art Nouveau-style café serves a generous breakfast. There's a quiet terrace in the inner courtyard.

 Kosy's
MAP Q5 ▪ Pariser Straße 50 ▪ Closed Sun

The name says it all: delicious cakes, pastries and hot chocolate served in a cosy atmosphere.

 POLKA Bar
MAP Q5 ▪ Pariser Straße 38 ▪ Open Thu–Sat

This bar, set in a basement vault, is the perfect venue in which to unwind and listen to music over a drink.

 Johanniscafé
MAP Q4 ▪ Johannisplatz 15

In a time-warped world of its own, the old-fashioned interior of this pub features a retro jukebox.

 Lollo Rosso
MAP Q5 ▪ Milchstraße 1

The so-called Bar(varian) Grill serves up a combination of Mediterranean and Bavarian favourites, from steaks to snacks, and a long drinks list.

Lollo Rosso Bar(varian) Grill interior

Restaurants

1 Bella Italia
MAP Q5 ▪ Weißenburger Straße 2 ▪ (089) 486179 ▪ €
Said to serve the best pizza in Munich. Outdoor tables are available.

2 Nana
MAP Q5 ▪ Metzstraße15 ▪ (089) 4449 9633 ▪ Closed Sun & Mon ▪ €
Bringing a touch of Tel Aviv flair to Munich, with delicious mezzes.

3 Le Faubourg
MAP Q4 ▪ Kirchenstraße 5 ▪ (089) 475533 ▪ Closed lunch, and Sun ▪ €€
A bistro atmosphere with bijou tables and specials presented on a chalkboard. Excellent wine selection. Limited outdoor tables available.

4 Rue des Halles
MAP Q4 ▪ Steinstraße 18 ▪ (089) 485675 ▪ Closed lunch ▪ €€
The oldest French establishment in the "French quarter", this unpretentious brasserie wouldn't look out of place among the old Parisian market halls. Innovative French cooking.

5 Bernard et Bernard
MAP Q4 ▪ Innere Wiener Straße 32 ▪ (089) 4 801173 ▪ Closed lunch ▪ €
What this crêperie lacks in size, it more than makes up for in quality, serving tasty crêpes, galettes and Breton-inspired dishes.

6 Nomiya Sushi Bar
MAP Q5 ▪ Wörthstraße 7 ▪ (089) 4 484095 ▪ Closed lunch ▪ €
Rustic cuisine with a Japanese/Bavarian twist. This restaurant is a strikingly unusual combination of sushi bar and pub.

Stone-baked pizza as served in Munich's Italian restaurants

7 Il Cigno
MAP R5 ▪ Wörthstraße 39 ▪ (089) 4 485589 ▪ Closed Sun ▪ €
Munich is mad about Italian food, and Il Cigno is a great place to enjoy pizza and pasta. Turn up in good weather and there will be outdoor seating available.

8 Chez Fritz
MAP Q4 ▪ Preysingstraße 20 ▪ (089) 4 487676 ▪ Closed lunch and Mon ▪ €€
This brasserie offers an upscale French menu with a retro atmosphere. Tables available on Preysingplatz.

Rue des Halles

9 Zum Kloster
MAP Q4 ▪ Preysingstraße 77 ▪ (089) 4 470564 ▪ €
This rustic eatery is the place to go for organic home cooking. Outdoor seating is available beneath cherry trees on a quiet street.

10 PreysingGarten
MAP Q4 ▪ Preysingstraße 69 ▪ (089) 6 886722 ▪ €
Breakfast (until 3pm), lunch and dinner are served Italian style at this wood-panelled venue. It also has an attractive garden and play area.

See map on p110

TOP10 South West

The area to the west and south of the old town is diverse and surprisingly green. Ludwigsvorstadt is the site of the huge Hauptbahnhof (main railway station) and Theresienwiese, the venue for the annual Oktoberfest. To the south of Sendlinger Tor and the Gärtnerplatz quarter, Isarvorstadt is home to a large number of shops and cafés, while the nearby Isar riverbanks offer a splendid backdrop. The Westend area, west of Theresienwiese, is a multicultural quarter that is undergoing rapid change, while the southwestern corner of this part of Munich is home to the green spaces of the Westpark.

Schönheit ("Beauty"),
Bavariapark

AREA MAP OF THE SOUTH WEST

1 Bavariapark
MAP J4–5

The park directly behind the Bavaria statue dates back to Ludwig I, who commissioned the creation of the "Theresienhain" (as it was then known) at the start of the 19th century. In 1872, the park was opened to the public and it later became an exhibition space when the Alte Messe events venue was established. Today, locals enjoy the park as somewhere to go jogging or to simply relax. It is home to a number of old stone sculptures as well as the Wirtshaus am Bavariapark with its attractive beer garden (see p125).

2 Altes Messegelände and Verkehrszentrum
MAP J4 ■ Am Bavariapark 5

Since the trade fair moved to Riem,

Vehicles at the Verkehrszentrum

the site of the Alte Messe (Old Fair) around Bavariapark and Theresienhöhe has undergone massive development. Contemporary residences have been built on the former exhibition grounds, including the tower of the Steidle-Haus, and many of the former exhibition halls have now been converted for cultural use. The Verkehrszentrum (a branch of the Deutsches Museum), which showcases the history of transport, is housed here in three protected Art Nouveau halls. Its permanent exhibition divides its collection of vehicles into three themes: urban transport, travel, and technology (see pp26–9).

3 Bavaria Statue and Theresienwiese
MAP JK4–5 ■ Theresienhöhe 16 ■ Apr–mid-Oct: 9am–6pm daily (until 8pm during Oktoberfest) ■ Adm

Standing 18.5 m (61 ft) tall, the bronze statue of *Bavaria* towers over her surroundings. She holds an oak wreath in her hand, while a lion sits at her feet. Designed by Ludwig Schwanthaler and cast by Ferdinand von Miller from 1840 to 1850, the statue was a masterpiece of technological achievement at the time, incorporating an observation platform in its head. Leo von Klenze's Ruhmeshalle (Hall of Fame), with busts honouring famous Bavarians, stands behind the colossal figure. *Bavaria* overlooks Theresienwiese, home of many events – most notably

the Oktoberfest *(see pp34–5)*. A festival was held here on 12 October 1810 to celebrate the wedding of crown prince Ludwig and Therese von Sachsen-Hildburghausen. In honour of the bride, the festival ground was named Theresienwiese.

4 Flaucher
MAP E6

This is Munich's best beach by the Isar. Every summer, sun worshippers flock to the gravel banks along the southern Isar, and many stop in at the pretty beer garden of the same name.

5 Westend
MAP J3–4

The Westend area (officially known as Schwanthalerhöhe after sculptor Ludwig von Schwanthaler) developed with the start of industrialization. Long considered a "Glasscherben-viertel" (broken glass, or pub district) with a multicultural vibe, it is now a

Mascot in action at the Audi Dome

real mix of old and new. The relocation of the trade fair gave rise to the construction of new residential areas, although the neighbourhood still retains some original buildings. Traditional pubs and shops sit beside chic cafés and stylish boutiques.

6 Audi Dome
MAP C6 ■ Grasweg 74 ■ Adm ■ www.fcb-basketball.de

The Rudi-Sedlmayer-Halle was built in 1972 as a basketball venue for the Olympic Games. It then hosted rock concerts, trade fairs and boxing events, and has been home to the Bayern Munich basketball club since becoming the Audi Dome in 2011.

7 Alte Kongresshalle
MAP J4 ■ Theresienhöhe 15

Originally built in 1952–3 in retro-futuristic style, the Old Congress Hall is one of a number of buildings that survived from the former exhibition grounds. Equipped with state-of-the-art technology, it often hosts cultural and social events. The hall's former teahouse is home to the Kongress Bar, while the Wirtshaus am Bavariapark can be found at the south end of the site *(see p125)*.

8 Tierpark Hellabrunn
MAP E7 ■ Tierparkstraße 30 ■ (089) 625080 ■ Open summer: 9am–6pm daily (winter: until 5pm) ■ Adm ■ www.hellabrunn.de

When Hellabrunn was founded in 1911, it was the first zoo in the world

Steidle-Haus in Westend

to arrange its 750 animals according to their geographic origins. Highlights include the jungle tent with its feline predators, a tropical forest and aquarium pavilion (where monkeys, snakes and fish inhabit a jungle and coral-reef habitat), the giraffe savannah and the ape enclosure.

9 Westpark
MAP BC6

A smaller, Westend version of the Englischer Garten, Westpark was created for the fourth International Horticultural Exposition in 1983. Among its attractions are landscaped gardens, barbecue and picnic facilities, two large lakes, and two beer gardens. The Asian section with its Japanese garden and Thai *sala* (pavilion) is especially beautiful.

Thai pavilion with Buddha statue, Westpark

10 Paulskirche
MAP K4 ■ St-Pauls-Platz 11

The view over the Wiesn (annual site of the Oktoberfest) from the 97-m (318-ft) high tower of this Neo-Gothic church is simply glorious, once you've conquered the 252 steps. St Paul's was the scene of tragic events in 1960, when a US military aircraft hit the tower and crashed down on a tram, shortly after take-off from Munich-Riem airport.

A DAY IN WESTEND

▶ **MORNING**

Begin at the **Bavaria** statue. Climb up to the head and enjoy the glorious view across Theresienwiese. Behind the Ruhmeshalle is the attractive **Bavariapark**. Walk through to its northern end and visit the **Verkehrszentrum** (Transport Centre), a branch of the Deutsches Museum housed in three halls. Cross Heimeranstraße and follow the tree-lined passage to Kazmairstraße (check out the beautiful sgraffito at no. 21). Just a few houses further down on the left, you'll find SchokoAlm (Kazmairstraße 33), which serves delicious coffee, cocoa, chocolates, gingerbread and cake. Next, take a stroll through the up and coming Westend quarter from Gollierplatz to Georg-Freundorfer-Platz. For lunch, try Marais (Parkstraße 2) or La Kaz (Kazmairstraße 38).

AFTERNOON

Head back through Bavariapark, and across the **Quartiersplatz Theresienhöhe** (over the S-Bahn) to reach the eastern section of **Westpark**. Stroll westwards until you come to "Die Arche" by Steffen Schuster, with a whole host of colourful animals. Making your way past the turtles in the **Mollsee**, past the Audi Dome and over the bridge (Mittlerer Ring), you will soon reach the western section of the park, which is home to a Thai sala, Chinese and Japanese garden, rose garden and a lake complete with a stage for open-air performances. If you're ready for a coffee or beer, call in at the See-Café or the **Wirtshaus am Rosengarten** restaurant.

See map on pp118–19 ←

The Best of the Rest

1 Hackerbrücke
MAP K3

One of the few wrought-iron arch bridges in Germany, the Hacker-brücke crosses the tracks in front of the Hauptbahnhof (train station; also the site of the central bus terminal).

2 Hauptzollamt
MAP C4 ■ Landsberger Straße 124

The main customs office, with its Jugendstil elements and glass dome, dates back to 1912.

3 Georg-Freundorfer-Platz
MAP J4

This square with a football pitch, summer curling and a climbing garden is a popular hang-out.

4 Endlose Treppe
MAP J4 ■ Ganghoferstraße 29

Olafur Eliasson's *Endlose Treppe* (Endless Staircase) is located in the courtyard of the KPMG offices.

5 Quartiersplatz Theresienhöhe
MAP J5

This concrete ceiling above the railway tracks was designed in 2010

Olafur Eliasson's *Endlose Treppe*

Quartiersplatz, Theresienhöhe

as a landscape sculpture, complete with hills, dunes and a play area.

6 Augustiner-Bräu
MAP J3 ■ Landsberger Straße 35

Munich's oldest brand of beer is brewed in the brickwork Augustiner brewery, which also has its own restaurant, the Augustiner Bräustuben (*see p125*).

7 Alter Südfriedhof
MAP LM3-6

Many prominent figures are buried at the city's oldest central cemetery. Today, local residents like to take a stroll under its ancient trees.

8 Central Tower
MAP D4 ■ Landsberger Straße 110

This distinctive, 23-storey building is one of Munich's few skyscrapers.

9 ADAC Zentrale
MAP C5 ■ Hansastraße 19

This showstopper Westend building (93 m/305 ft tall) features over 1,000 windows that shimmer in 22 colours. It is home to ADAC, the German motoring organization.

10 Gollierplatz
MAP D5

This beautiful, tree-lined square at the heart of Westend boasts a number of Jugendstil houses and the Neo-Romanesque St Rupert's church.

Cafés and Pubs

1 Lohner und Grobitsch
MAP D5 ■ Sandtnerstraße 5

This former grocery shop is now a café that still retains some of its old charm. Good cakes, as well as breakfast and salads.

2 Café Westend
MAP D5 ■
Ganghoferstraße 50

This combined café, bar and restaurant serves a great-value business lunch. It also has pool tables and bowling alleys in the basement.

3 Marais
MAP J3 ■ Parkstraße 2

A former shop with a nostalgia-inducing interior, including wooden chests and toy prams. Guests can drink coffee in the window display.

4 Café am Beethovenplatz
MAP L4 ■ Goethestraße 51

This traditional café, in a listed Belle Époque house belonging to the Hotel Mariandl, offers a real taste of Viennese coffee-house culture. There is live classical or jazz music every day and a small garden to enjoy in summer.

5 Aroma Kaffeebar
MAP M5 ■ Pestalozzistraße 24

This hipster café in a former pawn shop is located in the Glockenbach quarter. In addition to coffee and cakes, there is a selection of light meals available. The café also has its own shop, which stocks a real mishmash of fun products.

6 München 72
MAP M5 ■ Holzstraße 16

Named in memory of the attack at the 1972 Olympics, this café bar is brimming with 1970s furnishings – including a bicycle hanging behind the bar. Popular with mums in the afternoons, München 72 draws in a more varied crowd in the evening. The long-running German TV crime show *Tatort* is screened here on Sundays.

7 Tagträumer
MAP L6
■ Dreimühlenstraße 17

This coffee shop in the Schlachthof quarter is steeped in history –it was previously a police station and a butcher's shop, to name just two of its former incarnations – and is an atmospheric place for breakfast.

Cocktail

8 Substanz
MAP K6 ■
Ruppertstraße 28

This long-established pub, bar and live club host famous bands and newcomers alike, not to mention monthly poetry slams. It's very popular, so arrive early to get a seat.

Bar and seating area at Ferdings

9 Ferdings
MAP M5 ■ Klenzestraße 43
■ Closed Sun & Mon

Don't be put off by the bathrobes in the cloakroom – they are provided to keep smokers warm outside. This industrial bar serves regional tapas and a great selection of drinks.

10 Café Mozart
MAP L4 ■ Pettenkoferstraße 2

This café-restaurant with 1960s decor serves breakfast, as well as dinner and cocktails in the evening.

See map on pp118–19

Shops

 Comic Dealer
MAP J4 ▪ Gollierstraße 16

A comic shop that also sells manga, T-shirts, posters, models and more.

 WARE FREUDE
MAP C5 ▪ Westendstraße 142

T-shirts, postcards and decorative items – this place is perfect for souvenir shopping. The brand is synonymous with regional design and ecological production.

 SchokoAlm
MAP J4 ▪ Kazmairstraße 33

When it comes to chocolate, this chocolatier offers everything you could dream of and more, including tempting truffles, sweets and pastries, and gorgeous cakes. It also has its own café with some limited outdoor seating.

 louloute
MAP J4 ▪ Gollierstraße 33

With sewing courses on offer for beginners and pros alike, anyone can make a piece they'll love under expert guidance – alternatively, you can buy items from their collection.

Colourful trinkets on offer at Roly Poly

 Roly Poly
MAP M5 ▪ Klenzestraße 63

This designer fabric shop sells organic materials, accessories and also offers sewing courses. If you're into needlecraft, then it's definitely worth a visit.

Shop window, Götterspeise

 Götterspeise
MAP M5 ▪ Jahnstraße 30

The number-one hangout for chocolate fans in the Glockenbach quarter, this shop offers a whole host of tasty treats, vegan and lactose-free goodies, and gifts. The café serves cakes, pastries and coffee.

 Antonetty
MAP M5 ▪ Klenzestraße 56

Bags, clothes and a variety of other items made of leather are to be found in this shop. The little leather animals make good gifts.

 Rocket
MAP N5 ▪ Reichenbachstraße 41

This shop stocks the latest street-wear, shoes, accessories, bags and jewellery for adults and children.

Wohnpalette
MAP M5 ▪ Fraunhoferstraße 13

If you're shopping for picture frames, metal signs, decorative lighting or candlesticks, then you need look no further than Wohnpalette.

 Isarflimmern
MAP M5 ▪ Auenstraße 2

A cosy bookshop that's great for browsing. It also offers regular readings and "after-hours nights".

Restaurants

1 Augustiner Bräustuben
MAP J3 ▪ Landsberger
Straße 19 ▪ (089) 507047 ▪ €

A traditional Bavarian tavern at the
heart of the Augustiner brewery.

2 Wirtshaus am Bavariapark
MAP J4 ▪ Theresienhöhe 15
▪ (089) 45 211691 ▪ €

A great pub with an attractive beer
garden at the edge of Bavariapark.

3 Heimat Food
MAP J3 ▪ Schwanthalerstraße
149 ▪ (089) 23 239665 ▪ Closed Mon
▪ €€

Head chef Karl Ederer serves up
sophisticated regional cuisine.

4 Speiselokal Lenz
MAP K4 ▪ Pettenkoferstraße 48
▪ (089) 55 239771 ▪ €

This restaurant near Theresienwiese
serves international food for lunch
and dinner. Outdoor seating available.

5 Paulaner Bräuhaus
MAP L6 ▪ Kapuzinerplatz 5
▪ (089) 5 446110 ▪ €

This traditional brewery tavern has a
bar, lounge areas and a beer garden.

6 La Kaz
MAP J4 ▪ Ligsalzstraße 38
▪ (089) 76 990710 ▪ Closed Mon–Fri,
lunch ▪ €

Customers at this popular,
independently owned pub perch

PRICE CATEGORIES

Price of a three-course meal (or similar)
for one with a glass of wine or beer,
including taxes and service.

€ below €30   €€ €30–60   €€€ over €60

on colourful stools at wooden
tables to enjoy well-chilled wines
and excellent food.

7 Wirtshaus im Schlachthof
MAP L6 ▪ Zenettistraße 9 ▪ (089) 72
018264 ▪ Closed lunch, Tue except for
events ▪ €

This tavern with a beer garden and
stage hosts a range of events.

8 Itxaso Tapas
MAP M5 ▪ Pestalozzistraße 7
▪ (089) 23 708048 ▪ Closed Sun, lunch
Mon–Fri ▪ €

Possibly the most authentic
Spanish tapas bar in the city.

9 Grill & Grace
MAP C5 ▪ Guldeinstraße 50 ▪
(089) 14 348940 ▪ Closed Mon–Fri and
lunch ▪ €€

A steakhouse where guests get to
cook their own steaks on a lava-
stone grill.

10 Stemmerhof
MAP D6 ▪ Plinganserstraße 6
▪ (089) 74 654399 ▪ €

This urban yet rural place in a former
farmyard, serves European favourites.

Munich-style industrial chic at La Kaz

See map on pp118–19

TOP 10 North West

West of Maxvorstadt, Munich's northwest includes the districts of Neuhausen and Nymphenburg. The Hirschgarten – Bavaria's largest beer garden and a must for beer connoisseurs – is located in the far west of this part of the city. The Olympiapark and its varied attractions are located to the north, rubbing shoulders with one of Munich's largest companies, BMW, whose museum and BMW Welt attractions lie close to the car-maker's state-of-the-art plant.

Peony bloom

AREA MAP OF THE NORTH WEST

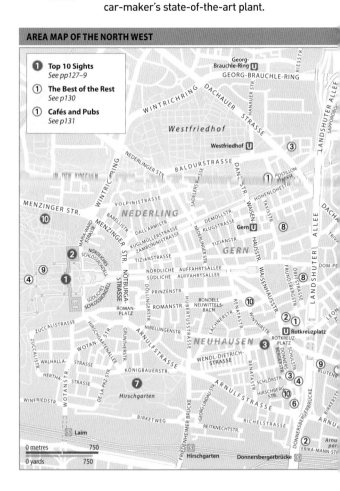

1 Top 10 Sights
See pp127–9

1 The Best of the Rest
See p130

1 Cafés and Pubs
See p131

1 Schloss Nymphenburg

Originally built as the 17th-century summer palace of Elector Ferdinand and Adelaide of Savoy, but much expanded since, Schloss Nymphenburg is one of the best places to escape the bustle of the city centre. Once you've toured the palace's many rooms, spend some time in the magnificent landscaped gardens, which are dotted with pavilions. Nymphenburg is famous for its porcelain, and a factory shop is located just outside the Schloss entrance. There are also a couple of museums in the palace

Schloss Nymphenburg

wings that are worth a visit, and there's an excellent café-restaurant where you can refuel (see p93).

2 Museum Mensch und Natur

MAP B2 ▪ (089) 1 795890 ▪ Open 9am–5pm Tue–Fri (until 8pm Thu), 10am–6pm Sat & Sun ▪ Adm ▪ DA ▪ www.mmn-muenchen.de

Located in a separate wing of the Schloss Nymphenburg, this museum guides you on a journey through biological, earth and life sciences, as you discover the history of Earth and life as we know it through dioramas, natural objects and interactive exhibits. One of the real stars of the exhibition is Bruno, the bear who wandered over the Alps into Bavaria from Italy in 2006 and was ultimately shot, despite protests.

3 Neuhausen

MAP CD3–4

Rotkreuzplatz is the centre of Munich's second-largest urban district, with countless bars and restaurants lining the streets surrounding the square. The many old buildings make it a popular residential area, and the quality of life here is excellent thanks to the multitude of green spaces such as the Botanischer Garten, Schlosspark Nymphenburg and the Hirschgarten.

4 Circus Krone
MAP K2 ▪ Zirkus-Krone-Straße 1–6 ▪ Tickets: (0) 1805 247287

While the circus is off touring in the summer, the Circus Krone Building doubles up as a venue for concerts and other events. Circus season traditionally begins on Christmas Day and offers three different shows until the end of February.

5 Olympiapark
Created in north Schwabing for the 1972 Summer Olympics, this site is the top sport and recreational ground in Munich (see pp32–3).

6 Sea Life
Bavaria's best aquarium can be found at the Olympiapark and it's a popular destination for visitors of all ages. One of the highlights is the shark tunnel (see p51).

Performer at Circus Krone's annual Christmas show

One of Sea Life's many sharks

7 Hirschgarten
MAP B3–4 ▪ Hirschgarten 1 ▪ (089) 17 999119 ▪ Open 10am–midnight (beer garden from 11:30am) ▪ www.hirschgarten.de

Located to the south of Schloss Nymphenburg, this beer garden is home to its own fallow deer enclosure, a nod to the park's former function as an electoral hunting ground (from 1780). A new hunting lodge was built in 1791 and became a popular destination for locals – particularly when it was licensed to sell beer. This was the first step in the venue becoming the tavern it is today, although it's probably best known for its huge beer garden that can seat up to 8,000 people, and where customers enjoy Augustiner beer in the shade of the chestnut trees. The 40-ha (99-acre) park is a much-loved site for sport and relaxation, including playgrounds, hills for tobogganing, and barbecue pits.

8 BMW Museum
MAP E1 ▪ Am Olympiapark 2 ▪ Open 10am–6pm Tue–Sun ▪ Adm ▪ (089) 1 2501 6001 ▪ DA ▪ www.bmw-welt.com

At the foot of the four-cylinder BMW Headquarters lies the bowl-shaped

Classic car at the BMW Museum

BMW Museum. This flat-roofed building is home to a permanent exhibition featuring over 120 cars, motorbikes and engines spanning nine decades of BMW history, while the "bowl" hosts changing exhibits.

9 BMW Welt
MAP E1 ■ Am Olympiapark 1 ■ (089) 1 2501 6001 ■ Building open 7:30am–midnight daily (Sun from 9am); exhibitions: 9am–6pm ■ DA ■ www.bmw-welt.com

This prestigious BMW building has been a prominent feature at Olympia-park since 2007. As the car manufacturer's distribution and experience centre, it has become one of the most popular attractions in Munich. Its distinctive double-cone design houses several exhibitions, as well as hosting political, art and cultural events. As well as its many shops, you can also find several restaurants here, including EssZimmer – home of top chef Bobby Bräuer.

BMW Welt and the BMW Museum

10 Botanischer Garten
MAP A2 ■ Menzinger Straße 65 ■ (089) 17 861316 ■ Open Jan, Nov & Dec: 9am–4:30pm daily; Feb, Mar & Oct: until 5pm; Apr & Sep: until 6pm; May, Jun, Jul & Aug: until 7pm ■ Adm ■ www.botmuc.de

Around 14,000 plant species from across the globe are cultivated outdoors and in greenhouses in these botanical gardens, which were laid out at the start of the 20th century. Highlights include the Alpinum and its alpine flora, the Arboretum with trees from around the world, June's spectacular rhododendron display, the fern glen, an insect pavilion full of butterflies and the greenhouses.

A DAY IN THE NORTH WEST

▶ MORNING

Start the day at **Schloss Nymphenburg**. Depending on the weather, you can enjoy a relaxed stroll through the Schlosspark or else marvel at the palace interior. Once you're ready for a coffee break, head into the **Schlosscafé im Palmenhaus**. Note that Nymphenburg is home to a couple of interesting museums, such as the **Museum Mensch und Natur** (in the palace wings). Once you're done here, wander down Auffahrtsallee towards Nymphenburger Straße and stop for lunch at the **Volkart** tapas bar on Volkartstraße.

AFTERNOON

From Nymphenburger Straße, it isn't far to Rotkreuzplatz. From here, take tram 12 (towards Scheidplatz) as far as Infanteriestraße and head down Ackermannstraße. You'll reach the **Olympiapark** in no time, where you can marvel at the architecture of the Olympic buildings. Don't forget to take in the view from the **Olympiaturm** – on a clear day you'll be able to see distant mountains. Once you've made your way back down to earth, there's plenty more exciting architecture to enjoy with **BMW Welt** waiting for you on the other side of the street. There's even the opportunity to make a quick detour to the **BMW Museum**, if you're interested. After a busy day's sightseeing, you can round things off at the exquisite EssZimmer restaurant at BMW Welt (tel (089) 3 5899 1814 for reservations) or the revolving restaurant at the top of the Olympiaturm.

See map on pp126–7 ←

The Best of the Rest

Dantebad in the stadium

① Dantebad
MAP C2 ▪ Postillonstraße 17 ▪
Open summer: 9am–8pm daily; rest of year: to 6pm ▪ www.swm.de
This open-air facility has more pools than any other swimming site in Munich. There's also a heated zone to enjoy in winter.

② Freiheiz
MAP D4 ▪ Rainer-Werner-Fassbinder-Platz 1
The renovated hall of this former thermal power station is a popular venue for concerts and events.

③ Borstei
MAP C1 ▪ Dachauer Straße 140
With its courtyards, gardens and fountains, this residential area was built in 1924–9 as an alternative to house sharing – a mini village within the city, complete with a museum.

④ Nymphenburger Kanal
MAP A–C3
Schloss Nympenburg's canal was commissioned by Max Emanuel in 1701. The section in front of the palace is a popular spot for curling when it freezes over in winter.

⑤ Reithalle
MAP E3 ▪ Heßstraße 132
The Neo-Romanesque former stables is now used to host events including the Opernfestspiele, theatre performances and concerts.

⑥ Olympiaturm
At 290 m (951 ft), the Olympic tower – and its view – are not to be missed (see pp32–3).

⑦ Augustiner-Keller
MAP K2 ▪ Arnulfstraße 52
This historic restaurant has a beer garden filled with old chestnut trees. Augustiner Edelstoff is served on tap.

⑧ Taxisgarten
MAP C2 ▪ Taxisstraße 12
This beer garden has existed since 1924 and hosts brass band performances at the weekend.

⑨ Schlosscafé im Palmenhaus
MAP A3 ▪ Schloss Nymphenburg, entrance 43 ▪ 11am–6pm Tue–Fri ▪ www.palemnhaus.de
A former greenhouse, this building is now a bright and airy café-restaurant with tables in the garden.

⑩ Herz-Jesu-Kirche
MAP C3 ▪ Lachnerstraße 8
Built in the late 1990s, this church resembles a semi-transparent cube with a blue front, while the interior features a free-standing wooden cube with slats that create different light effects.

The modern Herz-Jesu-Kirche

Cafés and Pubs

1 **The Victorian House**
MAP C3 ▪ Ysenburgstraße 13
▪ Closes 7pm Sun

A British venue offering a fusion of new and traditional English cuisine from breakfast through to dinner. It goes without saying that there's afternoon tea. Fabulous terrace.

2 **Volkart**
MAP C3 ▪ Volkartstraße 15
▪ Closed lunch, Sun

Tapas and Mexican cuisine are what it's all about here, including a wide variety of vegetarian options. Outdoor tables are available.

3 **Caffé Hausbrandt**
MAP C3 ▪ Schlörstraße 11

The Hausbrandt Trieste roasting house is considerably older than the Italian company illy, and this small coffee bar on Rotkreuzplatz is a great place to enjoy the perfect cup. You can also buy freshly roasted coffee and espresso machines here.

4 **Cafe Neuhauser**
MAP C3 ▪ Schulstraße 28

This modern neighbourhood cafe-bar serves everything from late breakfasts to last cocktails. The extensive menu includes around 50 different types of pizza and some delicious pasta dishes.

5 **Café Kosmos**
MAP L2 ▪ Dachauer Straße 7
▪ Closed Sat & Sun lunch

A bar with retro charm and a spiral staircase in an otherwise run-down area by the Hauptbahnhof. Normally very busy.

6 **Piacere Nuovo**
MAP C4 ▪
Donnersbergerstraße 54 ▪ Closed Sun, dinner Mon

Whether it's lunch or dinner you're after, you're in the right place for delicious home-made Italian specialities and wonderfully friendly service.

7 **Butter**
MAP J1 ▪ Blutenburgstraße 90
▪ Closed Sun

A great little bistro serving breakfasts, pastries and flavoursome mains.

8 **Café Ruffini**
MAP C3 ▪ Orffstraße 22–4
▪ Closed Mon

This Munich institution was the city's first eco café, serving up tasty organic treats, including wholesome breakfasts and baked goods from its own bakery. Sit on the rooftop terrace, where readings are occasionally held.

Organic café Ruffini

9 **Café Neuhausen**
MAP D3 ▪
▪ Blutenburgstraße 106

Breakfast, lunch and dinner (plus Sunday brunch) are served at this café with its stuccoed ceiling and covered garden. The menu comprises Italian, Austrian and Bavarian dishes.

10 **Sappralott**
MAP C3 ▪ Donnersbergerstr. 37

This Augustinian guesthouse with dark wood panelling serves Bavarian and international cuisine. Happy hour is from 11pm.

See map on pp126–7

📱10 Beyond Munich

Munich is the ideal starting point for excursions to the Upper Bavarian lakes – Ammersee and Starnberger See are the two main lakes in Fünfseenland – or to Chiemsee, known as the "Bavarian Sea". Also within easy reach are a number of ancient monasteries and world-famous churches, including the Wieskirche, a UNESCO World Heritage Site. A visit to at least one of Ludwig's palaces, preferably Neuschwanstein, is essential. It's worth noting that the Alps aren't just for hikers; you can easily reach Germany's highest peak – Zugspitze – in a day, via mountain railway and cable car.

Visitors at the top of the Zugspitze, Germany's highest peak

AREA MAP OF BEYOND MUNICH

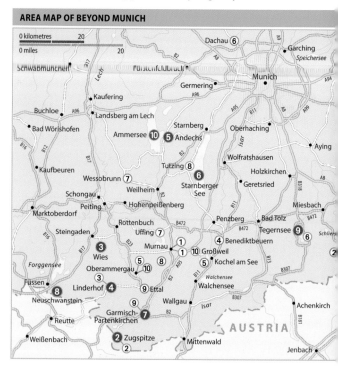

Chiemsee with a view of the mountains and islands

① Chiemsee, Herren-chiemsee and Fraueninsel

Popularly thought of as the "Bavarian Sea", Chiemsee is Bavaria's largest lake, with an area of 80 sq km (31 sq miles). It is home to four islands, the largest of which are Herreninsel and Fraueninsel – the latter boasts an 8th-century monastery. It is at Herrenchiemsee that you will find the Altes Schloss, an Augustinian monastery, and the Neues Schloss (Schloss Herrenchiemsee), which is said to be Ludwig II's Bavarian equivalent of Versailles. Despite construction beginning in 1878, the Neues Schloss was never completed. Its extravagant staircase and large mirror gallery are particularly impressive. The south wing is home to the King Ludwig II Museum (open daily, visit www.herrenchiemsee.de for details).

② Zugspitze

One of the best ways to enjoy the Zugspitze is to take a round trip on the mountain train and cable car. In Garmisch, the journey begins with the funicular, which takes you to the Schneeferner glacier on the Zugspitzplatt. Here, you switch to a cable car, which ascends to the summit. The observation platform offers a spectacular vista, and on a clear day you can see all the way to the Dolomites. Take the cable car on your way back down to the valley, and you'll be treated to wonderful views of Eibsee, Garmisch-Partenkirchen and Werdenfelser Land.

Rococo interior of the Wieskirche, a UNESCO World Heritage Site

③ Wieskirche
Wies 14, Steingaden ▪ (088) 62 932930 ▪ Open summer: 8am–8pm daily; winter: 8am–5pm daily ▪ www.wieskirche.de

Known simply as the Wieskirche, the mid-18th-century Pilgrim Church of the Scourged Saviour is renowned as a prime example of German Rococo. It represents the work of Dominikus Zimmermann at his peak. UNESCO listed the church as a World Heritage Site in 1983.

Ludwig II's Schloss Linderhof

④ Schloss Linderhof
Linderhof 12, Ettal ▪ (088) 2292030 ▪ Open Apr–mid-Oct: 9am–6pm daily; mid-Oct–Mar: 10am–4pm daily ▪ Adm ▪ www.schlosslinderhof.de

Schloss Linderhof was originally a hunting lodge belonging to

Maximilian II. Ludwig II had it torn down and rebuilt in the park, making it the only palace that was actually completed during his lifetime. The Schlosspark comprises a French garden complete with parterres and terraces, surrounded by a country park. It is home to attractions such as the Marokkanische Haus, Maurische Kiosk, and the famous Venus Grotto (closed for renovation until 2021), where the king liked to be rowed around in a golden boat.

⑤ Kloster Andechs
www.andechs.de

This "holy mountain" stands almost 200 m (656 ft) tall on the east bank of the Ammersee. Founded in 1455 as a Dominican monastery with a Rococo church, it is one of the most significant pilgrimage sites in Bavaria. Its tavern and beer garden attract crowds wanting to try the famous monastery beer, Andechser.

⑥ Starnberger See
Of all the lakes in this area, it was the Starnberger See (21 km/ 13 miles long, 5 km/3 miles wide and up to 127 m/417 ft deep) that became the most popular with the local population. Just like Ammersee, Tegernsee and Königssee, this lake is also home to tour boats from the "Weißblaue Flotte" fleet. Boasting a beautiful rose garden, the Roseninsel is the only island in the middle of the lake and can be easily reached with smaller boats. The lake

itself is surrounded by a number of palaces: "Sisi-Schloss" Possenhofen, Tutzing, Ammerland, and Berg, which was the summer house of the Wittelsbachs. It was near Berg that Ludwig II died under mysterious circumstances just a few metres from the shore, and a memorial cross marks the tragic spot in the lake. The Expressionist collection at the Buchheim Museum (the Museum der Phantasie), north of Bernried, is well worth a visit.

7 Garmisch-Partenkirchen

Located at the base of the Wetterstein massif and the Zugspitze, the capital of Werdenfelser Land is one of the most popular winter sports resorts in the country. In fact, the Winter Olympics were held here in 1936, as were the FIS Alpine World Ski Championships in 1978 and 2011. The buzzing spa town also draws a large number of visitors during the summer months, as its prime location makes it an ideal base for mountain hiking and excursions into the wider region. The town is light on sights, but the main draw here is without doubt the train and cable car ride up Zugspitze.

8 Neuschwanstein

Ludwig II's fairy-tale castle is not to be missed *(see pp36–7)*.

9 Tegernsee and Schliersee

Framed by wooded mountains, Tegernsee is one of the largest mountain lakes in Upper Bavaria, with an area of 9 sq km (3.5 sq miles). Its beautiful setting and proximity to Munich have made it a perennially popular holiday destination. Although not as well known, Schliersee is equally attractive. The best way to take in the scenery is with a walk around the lake (7 km/4 miles).

Water sports on the Ammersee

10 Ammersee

The Ammersee is the third-largest lake in Bavaria, occupying a glacial basin dating from the Ice Age. On a clear day, the view of the Alps is breathtaking. A variety of activities are available around the banks of the lake, including sailing, rowing, surfing, diving, cycling and walking.

Ludwig II's fairy-tale castle, Neuschwanstein

See map on pp132–3

The Best of the Rest

Wendelstein, a mountain with views as far as the Großglockner in Austria

1 Münter-Haus, Murnau
Kottmüllerallee 6, Murnau
◾ Open 2–5pm Tue–Sun ◾ Adm

The Münter-Haus was the summer house of Gabriele Münter and Wassily Kandinsky, and a meeting point for the "Blue Rider" artists.

2 Spitzingsee
This wildly romantic lake is part of the Spitzingsee–Tegernsee ski resort.

3 Wendelstein
This 1838-m (6030-ft) mountain peak can be reached via the 1912 rack railway, by cable car, or on foot.

4 Kloster Benediktbeuern
Don-Bosco-Straße 1, Benediktbeuern ◾ Tours 2:30pm daily

Benediktbeuern Abbey is one of the oldest monasteries in Germany, dating from 739. The library in the present Baroque complex was once home to the 13th-century *Carmina Burana* manuscript.

5 Kochelsee and Walchensee
The Kochelsee and the Walchensee further south are perfect for windsurfing. The Walchensee is the largest and deepest mountain lake in Germany (covering 16 sq km/6 sq miles, and up to 192 m/630 ft deep).

6 Dachau
Alte Römerstraße 75, Dachau
◾ (081) 31 669970 ◾ Open 9am–5pm daily ◾ www.kz-gedenkstaette-dachau.de

The first concentration camp was established in 1933 in Dachau (around 20 km/12 miles from Munich). Tours of the memorial site can be booked in advance.

7 Kloster Wessobrunn
Klosterhof 4, Wessobrunn ◾ www.kloster-wessobrunn.de

Wessobrunn stuccowork is internationally renowned. Parts of the monastery are open to the public.

8 Murnauer Moos
www.murnau.de

A boardwalk leads into the largest continuous moorland in Bavaria (32 sq km/12 sq miles).

9 Kloster Ettal
Kaiser-Ludwig-Platz 1, Ettal

Now a boarding school, this abbey is famous for its herbal liqueur (which can still be bought here).

10 Oberammergau
This health resort adorned with Lüftlmalerei frescos is world famous for its *Passionsspiele*, held every 10 years. The next ones are scheduled for 2020.

Restaurants

PRICE CATEGORIES
Price of a three-course meal (or similar)
for one, with a glass of wine or beer,
including taxes and service.

€ below €30   €€ €30–60   €€€ over €60

1 Alpenhof Murnau
Ramsachstraße 8, Murnau
■ (088) 41 491320 ■ DA ■ €€

Upscale Bavarian/international
restaurant with a panoramic view
of the Alps.

2 Gletscherrestaurant Sonnalpin
www.zugspitze.de ■ €

This restaurant on the Zugspitzplatt
glacial plateau is, at 2,600 m (8,530 ft),
the highest eatery in Germany.

3 Schlosshotel Linderhof
Linderhof 14, Ettal
■ (088) 22790 ■ €€

Bavarian specialities served against
the backdrop of Ludwig's palace.

4 Inselhotel zur Linde
Fraueninsel im Chiemsee
■ (080) 5 490366 ■ €€

This traditional, 600-year-old hotel
serves home-made cakes and
Bavarian specialities.

5 Hotel Alte Post
Dorfstraße 19, Oberammergau
■ (088) 229100 ■ €

Bavarian delicacies in the centre
of town, served inside and outdoors.

Herzogliches Bräustüberl Tegernsee

6 Herzogliches Bräustüberl Tegernsee
Schlossplatz 1, Tegernsee ■ (080)
224141 ■ €

A cosy and rustic Bavarian inn with
a lovely terrace.

7 Seerestaurant Alpenblick
Kirchtalstraße 30, Uffing ■ (088)
469300 ■ Winter: closed Sun ■ €€

The view of the Staffelsee from
the terrace and beer garden is
sensational. Great, seasonal food.

8 Wirtschaft zum Häring
Midgardstraße 3–5, Tutzing
■ (081) 581216 ■ Closed Mon
■ €€

Serving breakfast through to dinner
on the terrace overlooking Starnberg
See, in the beer garden, or in the
conservatory of Midgard-Haus.
The best strudel in town.

9 Gasthof zum Rassen
Ludwigstraße 45, Garmisch-
Partenkirchen ■ (088) 212089 ■ €

This traditional inn, serving classic
Bavarian fare, is home to Germany's
oldest folk theatre.

10 Kreut-Alm
Kreut 1, Großweil ■ (088)
415822 ■ €

This restaurant offers a breathtaking
panoramic view of the mountains. It
also has a terrace and beer garden.

Hotel Alte Post, Oberammergau

See map on pp132–3 →

Streetsmart

Westfriedhof U-Bahn station, with
lighting designed by Ingo Maurer

Getting To and Around Munich

Arriving by Air

Opened in 1992, **Munich Airport** is a major hub for air travel, with most international and domestic airlines passing through. It is equipped with hundreds of shops, restaurants and cafés, and a tourist information centre. Terminals 1 and 2 house the offices of over 100 airlines.

Conveniently located right on the A92, Munich Airport is around 28 km (17 miles) from the city centre. The S-Bahn (S1 & S8) will take you to Marienplatz or the Hauptbahnhof in 40 or 45 minutes, and taxis take the same time provided that the roads are clear.

If you'd like to hire a car, you can find most of the big international rental companies at the airport.

Arriving by Rail

Whether you're coming from Berlin, Rome, Paris, Vienna or Budapest, **München Hauptbahnhof** handles trains from every direction. In most cases, it also offers direct connections to major European cities several times a day. Southern Bavaria is extremely well connected thanks to its dense rail network.

Most German trains and railway lines are operated by **Deutsche Bahn AG**. Long-distance routes are served by InterCity Express (ICE), InterCity (IC) and EuroCity (EC) trains, while the network also runs Regional-Express (RE) and RegionalBahn (RB) for shorter distances. The S-Bahn suburban trains cover a radius of around 30–40 km (19–25 miles) around Munich.

Arriving by Bus

Many long-distance buses arrive at and depart from the central bus terminal – **Zentraler Omnibusbahnhof (ZOB)** – at the Hackerbrücke. Tourist hotspots in Upper Bavaria (and even some out-of-the-way destinations) are well served by a network of regional bus routes.

Arriving by Car

Six motorways lead into Munich: the A8 Stuttgart/ Salzburg, A95 Garmisch-Partenkirchen, A96 Lindau, A9 Nuremberg/ Berlin, A92 Deggendorf and A94 Passau. The Autobahnring ring road (A99, incomplete) enables you to bypass the city in part. If you plan to drive into the city, you will need to take two additional ring roads: the Mittlerer Ring and, once you reach the centre, the Altstadtring.

U-Bahn and S-Bahn

Constructed in 1968, the U-Bahn underground rail network runs modern and comfortable trains. Nearly all of its stations are wheelchair-accessible. Seven lines are currently in operation within the city zone (the U8 is only intended as a booster line). In total, the network spans over 100 km (62 miles) and comprises over 100 stations.

The S-Bahn suburban rail network radiates in a star shape from the city centre towards the neighbouring districts and is ideal for taking day trips to the lakes or to Dachau. The S-Bahn is also an important means of transport within the city centre: its central stretch (11 km/7 miles with all 7 lines) between Donnersbergerbrücke and Ostbahnhof (via Hauptbahnhof, Stachus and Marienplatz) offers connection points to the U-Bahn, buses and trams. The majority of S-Bahn stations are wheelchair-accessible.

Trams

Munich's tram network runs in part on accelerated routes. Some lines are perfect for sight seeing (19 goes through the old town, for example, and the 25 to Grünwald is a particularly scenic route). Most tram cars have ramps to allow wheelchair access.

Buses

Munich has two types of bus service: MetroBus for the main routes and StadtBus for connections to S-Bahn and U-Bahn services. StadtBus 100 (Museumslinie) runs past several museums. Some buses have low floors with ramps to assist wheelchair users.

Tickets

All public transport operated by the **MVV**

(Munich Traffic and Tariff Association) – U-Bahns, S-Bahns, trams and buses – use the same tickets. These can be bought at ticket machines in U-Bahn and S-Bahn stations, on trams and buses, or as a mobile ticket. Several ticket types are available: multi-ride (Streifenkarten), single-ride (Einzelkarten), daily passes (Tageskarten), weekly passes (Wochenkarten) and monthly passes (Monatskarten). Multi-ride tickets have to be validated for each zone (zone 1 is the central one). A normal journey uses 2 strips, while a short hop is 1 strip.

Visitors can take advantage of special rates, for example the **CityTour-Card**, which is available for individuals or groups (of up to 5 people; children count as a half person), is valid for all forms of public transport, and includes reduced entry to over 60 attractions. These tickets are available to buy at ticket machines, from tourist information centres or online.

Taxis

You can book a taxi by telephone, hail one or join a queue at a taxi rank. The minimum charge is €3.70, then €1.90 per km (€1.70/€1.60 after 5/10 km).

Cars

Getting around the city by car isn't a great choice: parking is difficult, and only cars approved as environmentally friendly (with a green sticker) are allowed within the Mittlerer Ring.

Bicycles

Munich is a bicycle-friendly city with plenty of cycle paths. Various bike- rental options are available, including the **MVG Rad** system, which provides 1,200 bicycles across 125 stations.

On Foot

Exploring the old town is best done on foot. Other areas that are easy to explore on foot include Schwabing, Haidhausen, Neuhausen, the banks of the Isar, and Westend.

Bayerische Seenschifffahrt

This fleet of vessels offers themed tours and excursions on Starnberger See, Ammersee, Königssee and Tegernsee.

DIRECTORY

BY AIR

Austrian
((069) 50 600598
w austrian.com

Lufthansa
((069) 86 799799
w lufthansa.com

Munich Airport
((089) 97500
w munich-airport.de

Swiss
((069) 86 798000
w swiss.com

BY RAIL

Deutsche Bahn AG
((0) 1806 996633
w bahn.de

München Hauptbahnhof
MAP L3 ■
Bayerstraße 10A

BY BUS

FlixBus
w flixbus.de

Regionalverkehr Oberbayern (regional transport)
w rvo-bus.de

Zentraler Omnibus-bahnhof (ZOB)
MAP K2 ■ Hackerbrücke 4
w muenchen-zob.de

BY CAR

ADAC Breakdown Service
((089) 222222

U-BAHN AND S-BAHN

CityTourCard
w citytourcard-muenchen.de

MVV/MVG
MAP N3 ■ Marienplatz
S-Bahn mezzanine
((0) 8003 4422 6600 (free hotline)
w mvv-muenchen.de

BUSES AND TRAMS
w mvg.de

TAXIS

IsarFunk
((089) 450540
w isarfunk.de

Taxi München eG
((089) 21610/19410
w taxi-muenchen.com

BICYCLES

Call a Bike
w bahn.de

MVG Rad (city cycle-hire system)
((0) 8003 4422 6622
w mvg.de

Pedalhelden
((089) 24 216880
w pedalhelden.de

BOATS

Bayerische Seenschifffahrt
((081) 518061
w seenschifffahrt.de

Practical Information

Customs and Immigration

Visitors from EU countries and Switzerland require a valid ID card or passport to enter Germany, and children of all ages must have their own photo ID. Germany has reinstated ad hoc passport checks at some of its land borders, so always make sure you have your ID with you.

There are no longer customs restrictions between member countries of the Schengen Area, meaning all goods for personal use may be imported and exported duty free.

Citizens of non-EU countries require a passport and, in some cases, also a visa. The **Federal Foreign Office** as well as the embassy or **consulate** of your home country can provide information on current customs regulations.

Travel Safety

Visitors can get up-to-date travel safety information from the **Foreign and Commonwealth Office** in the UK, the **State Department** in the US and the **Department of Foreign Affairs and Trade** in Australia.

Tourist Information

Munich's tourist board has two **tourist information centres**: one in the Rathaus on Marienplatz and the other at the Hauptbahnhof. Here, visitors can access all sorts of information and services, from brochures and city maps to tickets or room reservations. There's also another information centre at Alten Hof, as well as the main desk at Munich Airport.

If you are interested in visiting the surrounding countryside, local tourist offices in the various districts – for example in Garmisch-Partenkirchen (www.gapa.de) or Bad Tölz (www.bad-toelz.de) – are useful resources.

Personal Security

Munich has one of the lowest crime rates not only in Germany, but in the whole of Europe. You can therefore relax and enjoy your holiday, as long as you observe general safety measures.

Large groups of people are always a target for pickpockets wherever you go, and Munich is no exception. Be sure to stay vigilant at all times, particularly on crowded U-Bahns or S-Bahns, in the busy pedestrian zones, and especially at the Oktoberfest.

Medical Care

For EU citizens, the statutory health insurance of the respective country (**EHIC**) covers essential outpatient or inpatient medical treatment in Germany. For visitors from other countries, travel health insurance is strongly recommended. If your case is not an emergency, you should seek out a regular GP or dental practice during the week. Check the *Gelbe Seiten* (Germany's *Yellow Pages*) for addresses of all kinds of doctors. Most doctors and medical staff speak some English.

Hospitals and Chemists

Munich has an excellent hospital service. Some of the clinics attached to the university occupy a prime central location and even have emergency departments.

Chemists (pharmacies) are easy to spot with their big red "A" (for Apotheke) signs, and usually stay open until 7 or 8pm. After this time, every chemist displays the names and addresses of other chemists in the area offering an emergency evening or weekend service. You can also find details of the nearest chemist online.

Lost Property

If you leave something on the U-Bahn, tram or on the bus, try contacting the municipal lost property office or even the MVG (Munich Transport Corporation) lost-and-found service. If you've left something on the S-Bahn, contact the lost property point at the Hauptbahnhof. There is also a lost-and-found office at the airport.

Disabled Travellers

Several areas in Munich have original cobblestone paving, which may prove difficult for wheelchair users. Similarly, some restaurants in old buildings may only have limited access.

Most S-Bahn and U-Bahn stations in the city zone offer barrier-free access, and most trams have facilities to cater for those with special needs. Buses with low floors for easy access are designated as such. Public toilets with disabled access can be found in public transport stations. Details can be found in the MVV brochure "Barrierefrei" ("Barrier free"), available at MVV ticket kiosks.

The city's tourism website provides a list of venues with special access facilities, including hotels, restaurants, museums and swimming pools. You can also pick up relevant brochures from the tourist information points in Marienplatz and at the Hauptbahnhof.

When it comes to sightseeing, the local tourist board operates special city tours for the hearing impaired (also available in international sign language) and for visitors who are visually impaired or blind. Some tour operators, such as the **Weis(s)e Stadtvogel**

or Stattreisen München, provide tours for disabled visitors (see p147).

The **Club Behinderter und ihrer Freunde** (Club for the Disabled and Friends or **CBF**) provides information on cinemas, theatres, museums and other venues with access for people with disabilities. It also organizes events such as wheelchair rambles, offers support for cultural events, and can help find a doctor.

Addition information, advice and wheelchair rentals are also available from VDK Bayern (Munich information centre: (089) 2 117172, www.vdk.de).

DIRECTORY

CUSTOMS AND IMMIGRATION

Customs
🗔 zoll.de

Federal Foreign Office
🗔 auswaertiges-amt.de

CONSULATES

Austrian Consulate General
MAP H4 ▪ Ismaninger Straße 136 📞(089) 998150 🗔 bmeia.gv.at/gk-muenchen

Swiss Consulate General
MAP H4 ▪ Prinz-regentenstraße 20
📞 (089) 2 866200
🗔 eda.admin.ch/muenchen

TRAVEL SAFETY

Australia Department of Foreign Affairs and Trade
🗔 dfat.gov.au
🗔 smartraveller.gov.au

UK Foreign and Commonwealth Office
🗔 gov.uk/foreign-travel-advice

US Department of State
🗔 travel.state.gov

TOURIST INFORMATION

Hauptbahnhof
MAP L3 ▪ Bahnhofsplatz 2

Marienplatz
MAP N3 ▪ Neues Rathaus, Marienplatz 8
📞 (089) 23 396500

München Tourist board
MAP M4 ▪ Sendlinger Straße 1 🗔 muenchen.de

EMERGENCY NUMBERS

European emergency number (fire, rescue, ambulance)
📞 112

Police
📞 110

On-call Medical Service
📞 116 117

Women's Emergency Hotline
📞 (089) 763737

Emergency Dentist
📞 (089) 30 005515

HOSPITALS WITH EMERGENCY DEPARTMENTS

Chirurgische Klinik und Poliklinik

MAP L4
▪ Nußbaumstraße 20
📞 (089) 4 4005 2611

Klinikum Schwabing
MAP F1 ▪ Kölner Platz 1
📞 (089) 30680
För children/the young:
Parzivalstraße 16
📞 (089) 30 682589

EMERGENCY CHEMIST

🗔 lak-bayern.notdienst-portal.de

LOST PROPERTY

Airport
📞 (089) 97 521470

Hauptbahnhof
📞 (089) 13 086664

MVG Fundbüro
MAP C5
▪ Elsenheimerstraße 61
📞 (0) 8003 4422 6600

Städtisches Fundbüro
MAP C6
▪ Oetztaler Straße 19
📞 (089) 23 396045

DISABLED TRAVELLERS

CBF
MAP G2 ▪ Johann-Fichte-Straße 12
📞 (089) 3 568808

Currency and Banking

For visitors from the Eurozone, the days of changing currency are over. All other visitors can call in at bureau de change offices (at train stations, for example) or a bank to convert their currency to euros. Some money-changing machines are available in the city.

Central Munich has a large number of branches of all major banks. Most of these close around 4pm, although some stay open later for one day of the week. The ReiseBank at Munich Hauptbahnhof, for example, is open until 10pm (and until 9pm at the airport).

If you need to withdraw money, use one of the cashpoints (ATMs) dotted all over the city. Note that contactless withdrawals are not supported. Let your bank or credit card company know immediately if you lose your card or it is stolen, so that they can ensure it is blocked. The emergency blocking line is the central point of contact for blocking debit cards over the phone. Be aware that your bank will charge you for withdrawals, so taking out a couple of large sums is cheaper than lots of small withdrawals.

Credit and Debit Cards

Almost all hotels (with the exception of small B&Bs), department stores and larger shops, as well as many restaurants, accept major credit and debit cards, such as **Visa** and **MasterCard**. **American Express, Diners Club** and other cards are less widely accepted.

Small restaurants and beer gardens generally take cash only.

Telephone

Deutsche Telekom is the provider for public telephones. As most people now carry mobile phones, public pay phones are no longer as prevalent as they once were. Some phones accept credit cards or calling cards. Avoid making calls from hotel rooms, as they can be very expensive.

Network providers T-Mobile, Vodafone and O2 cover Munich and Bavaria, and coverage is generally good except in remote areas, such as in the Alps. Mobile phones can be used on the S-Bahn and even on the U-Bahn without any issues.

Internet and Wi-Fi

High-speed internet and Wi-Fi is available in cafés and hotels all across the city.

For anyone who likes to browse or blog on the move, Munich has 21 free Wi-Fi hotspots, including Marienplatz, Karlsplatz/Stachus, Odeonsplatz, Münchner Freiheit and the Deutsches Museum. Munich Wi-Fi (M-WLAN) is also offered with encryption; all you have to do is register once for free. The number of free Wi-Fi hotspots is constantly growing. Be aware that the German

for Wi-Fi is W-Lan (pronounced *veh-lan*).

Postal Services

Post offices in Munich are very much in decline, as retailers (partner branches) have started to take over the service. As a result, many of the large, architecturally interesting post office buildings of the past – such as the 19th-century Isarpost on Sonnenstraße or the 18th/19th-century Residenzpost (opposite the Residenz) – have been converted into shopping centres that include offices, restaurants and event venues.

Postcards cost €0.45 to send within Germany, and €0.90 internationally. Postage for letters is €0.70/€0.90.

Radio and Television

Munich is the biggest publishing city in Germany and a key media hub, with various radio and TV broadcasters – both public, such as Bayerische Rundfunk (BR), and private – established here.

Bayerische Rundfunk has five radio stations, and several independent stations also broadcast traffic and travel information, news and music. Around 50 channels are available in Munich via digital radio (DAB+ standard).

Newspapers and Magazines

The two big daily newspapers – the *Süddeutsche Zeitung (SZ)* and *Münchner Merkur* – also include local sections. You can also check out Munich's tabloids, *AZ* and *tz*, for details of local events.

Munich publishes two city magazines, the oldest of which is *In München*, available for free in pubs, shops and other popular locations. *In München* is published every fortnight and covers cinema, theatre, current events and more. The second city magazine is more of a lifestyle magazine, called *Monacao de Luxe*.

In addition to these, you will also find a whole host of Munich portals and blogs online covering general information along with more specific articles and reviews, for example on breakfast cafés.

Opening Hours

Most shops in the city centre are open Monday to Saturday, 9am to 8pm, although the subject of relaxing or even abolishing the law regulating opening hours is frequently under discussion. Offices, banks and post offices tend to close earlier, usually by 4, 5 or 6pm.

Tickets

Tickets for the theatre or music concerts can generally bought from the relevant ticket offices. Telephone numbers for these can be found throughout this guide.

Alternatively, **München Ticket** offers advance tickets for most events. Advance ticket points also exist at the Rathaus (town hall), Gasteig cultural centre, and the information pavilion at the Olympia Eishalle arena.

You will also find advance booking centres on the lower floor of the S-Bahn station at Marienplatz and on the lower floor of Stachus.

Time Zone

Munich uses Central European Time (CET), and Germany observes daylight-savings summer time from the end of March to the end of October, like its neighbouring countries.

When to Visit

Munich is a good destination at any time of the year. It goes without saying that the weather's at its best in spring, summer and autumn, although winter brings a number of cultural events, not to mention the chance to enjoy some winter sports in the ski resorts of the nearby Alps.

Visitors to Munich can enjoy beautifully sunny days in January. April is usually more variable, with May also flitting between warm summery and cold wintry temperatures. As May marks the official start of the beer garden season, this is when the first raft rides take place on the Isar. Munich's outdoor swimming venues reach their peak temperatures in August. It is not unknown for the region to experience Indian summers during the autumn, and this is its best time for hiking tours around the area. The notorious Föhn is a warm, dry, down-slope wind that sweeps over the area from the Alps.

Shopping

Fashion is very much concentrated in the city's central shopping areas – spanning the pedestrian zone of Sendlinger Straße (including Hofstatt), Maximilianstraße (Maximilianhöfen), Residenzstraße and Theatinerstraße (Fünf Höfen), as well as at the eastern end of Leopoldstraße and Hohenzollernstraße in Schwabing. If you're into young, quirky fashion, it's also worth giving Gärtner-platz a try (see p69).

The pedestrian zone is packed with branches of popular chain stores, such as **Zara**, along with department stores including **Galeria Kaufhof** and **Karstadt**.

Maximilianstraße is very much the city's luxury boulevard, with high-end designer brands such as Dolce & Gabbana, Chanel, Hermès, **Escada**, Gucci, Valentino, YSL, Dior and **Giorgio Armani**.

Music fans should definitely visit **Hieber Lindberg**, which offers a selection of interesting genres along with a wide range of sheet music. The CD section at Ludwig Beck on Rathauseck (see p85) has a broad selection of classical music and jazz.

In addition to Munich's eight branches of **Hugen-dubel**, you will also find a whole host of bookshops concentrated around the university. For second-hand books, **Antiquariat Kitzinger** is definitely worth a visit.

Summer and winter sales don't run in the same way they used to, although prices do tend to drop at the end of the season. There are also various discounts and special offers that run over the course of the year – just keep an eye out for the "Sale" signs.

The VAT (sales tax) rate in Germany is set at 19 per cent (or 7 per cent in some cases) and is generally included in the prices on display.

Restaurants

Restaurants generally open around lunchtime, but some don't open until the evening, about 6pm. Those that do serve lunch sometimes close again for a few hours in the afternoon, and those that are open in the evening usually run until midnight or later. Some even serve food into the small hours, although the inner-city beer gardens stop serving outside at 11pm. Most restaurants have their menus displayed outside.

Like most large cities, Munich offers all kinds of restaurants, from Middle Eastern to Polynesian, although Italian is a firm favourite with the locals.

Munich has been Germany's unofficial capital for decades, which explains why it has so many top restaurants and expensive places to be seen. Some of these spots are amongst the best in central Europe.

If you're looking for Bavarian specialities, the best places to try them are traditional taverns or restaurants run by breweries. Be sure to try Weißwurst (sausage), Schweinshaxe mit Knödeln (ham hock and dumplings) or Rostbratwürste mit Sauerkraut (barbecued sausages and cabbage), followed by the sweet treat of Bayrische Creme (Bavarian cream).

Traditional beer garden fare includes Obatzda (a spicy cheese spread) served with Breze (pretzels) and Bavarian Wurstsalat (sausage salad). Brotzeit (literally "bread time"), a traditional Bavarian dish, is a cold snack composed of sausage, bacon, cheese and radish.

It's always best to book a table in advance for fine-dining and Michelin-starred restaurants or popular pubs, especially if you're in a large group. It's also a good idea to book for weekends in general. Be warned that many traditional taverns have tables reserved for their regulars, known as "Stammtische". You should never sit at these.

It's worth noting that service is included in the bill in restaurants. If you must leave a tip, just round the bill up to the nearest €5.

City Tours and Excursions

A wide variety of tour operators offer city tours and excursions in various languages. Most of these tours start at the Haupt-bahnhof. **CitySightseeing** runs three combinable trips on a double-decker bus that operate on a hop-on, hop-off basis. **Gray Line** also offers hop-on tours, themed tours, and day trips, including to the Zugspitze and Neuschwanstein. You will also find smaller tours of specific areas of the city, as well as sightseeing by bike, Segway, rickshaw or carriage. A list of operators can be found on the München Tourismus website (see p143).

Guided Tours

A variety of companies offer themed tours of the city (covering topics such as Munich's Art Nouveau history, Jewish culture, beer, the Wittelsbachs, or specific districts), including special tours for people with disabilities. You can choose from cycle tours, tram tours, culinary tours, tours of Munich's film locations, tours of

mystical Munich, and "night watchman" tours, to name just a few. Alternatively, if you would prefer to take it all in from above, you can book a helicopter ride (list of operators available at www.muenchen.de).

Hotels

Hotel prices in Munich are generally higher than in the rest of Bavaria, although breakfast is often included. That said, there are still plenty of affordable places to stay, including small hotels, guesthouses, serviced apartments, B&Bs and homestays.

The number of stars provides an indication of a hotel's quality, but also of its price. Prices vary according to the season (during Oktoberfest is particularly expensive) and the amenities provided, although many hotels do have reduced weekend rates and lower prices during the off-season.

Bookings can be made over the phone or online with the specific hotel. München Tourismus also offers a free booking service, which can be accessed from the tourist information centres, online or by phone.

DIRECTORY

SHOPPING

Antiquariat Kitzinger
MAP N1
▪ Schellingstraße 25
📞 (089) 283537
🌐 antiquariat-kitzinger.de

Escada
MAP N3 ▪ Maximilianstraße 25
📞 (089) 2 199650
🌐 escada.com

Galeria Kaufhof
MAP N3 ▪
Kaufingerstraße 1–5
📞 (089) 231851
MAP L3 ▪ Karlsplatz 21–4
📞 (089) 51250
🌐 galeria-kaufhof.de

Giorgio Armani
MAP N3
▪ Maximilianstraße 32
📞 (089) 29 191120
🌐 armani.com

Hieber Lindberg
MAP L3
▪ Sonnenstraße 15
📞 (089) 551460
🌐 hieber-lindberg.de

Hugendubel
MAP M3 ▪ Karlsplatz 12

MAP N3
▪ Theatinerstraße 11
📞 (089) 30 757575
🌐 hugendubel.de

Karstadt
MAP M3
▪ Neuhauser Straße 20
📞 (089) 290230
MAP L3 ▪ Bahnhofplatz 7
📞 (089) 55120
🌐 karstadt.de

Zara
MAP M3
▪ Kaufingerstraße 14
📞 (089) 25 543830
MAP M3
▪ Neuhauser Straße 33
📞 (089) 23 077434
🌐 zara.com

GASTRO GUIDES

Munichx
🌐 munichx.de/essen

Süddeutsche Zeitung
🌐 sueddeutsche.de/thema/Restaurants

CITY TOURS AND EXCURSIONS

CitySightseeing
🌐 citysightseeing-muenchen.de

Gray Line
📞 (0) 7002 8786 8775
or (0) 8954 907560
🌐 grayline.de

GUIDED TOURS

Heliflieger
📞 (089) 4 1610 9180
🌐 heliflieger.com

Spurwechsel
📞 (089) 6 924699
🌐 spurwechsel-muenchen.de

Stattreisen München
📞 (089) 54 404230
🌐 stattreisen-muenchen.de

Weis(s)er Stadtvogel München
📞 (089) 2 0324 5360
🌐 weisser-stadtvogel.de

ACCOMMODATION

City Mitwohnzentrale
📞 (089) 592510
🌐 mitwohnzentrale.de

Mr. Lodge
🌐 mrlodge.de

Places to Stay

PRICE CATEGORIES
For a standard double room per night (with breakfast if included), taxes and service.

€ under €100 €€ €100–200 €€€ over €200

Luxury Hotels

Bayerischer Hof
MAP M3 ■ Promenadeplatz 2–6 ■ (089) 212 00 ■ www.bayerischerhof.de ■ Limited wheelchair access ■ €€€
Now in the hands of the fourth generation, this privately owned luxury hotel, dating back to 1841, offers 340 individually styled rooms and suites, 40 banquet rooms, five restaurants (the two-Michelin-starred Atelier, plus Garden, Palais Keller and Trader Vic's) and six bars.

The Charles Hotel
MAP L2 ■ Sophienstraße 28 ■ (089) 544 5550 ■ www.roccofortehotels.com ■ €€€
A member of the Rocco Forte group, this luxury five-star hotel can be found next to the Alter Botanischer Garten, not far from Karlsplatz. Built on the site of an old university library, rooms are modern and spacious. It also offers a restaurant with terrace, spa, gym and conference rooms.

Mandarin Oriental
MAP N3 ■ Neuturmstraße 1 ■ (089) 290980 ■ www.mandarinoriental.com ■ €€€
First-class service and historic ambience near Maximilianstraße. This five-star hotel has 53 rooms and 20 suites, as well as banqueting and conference facilities. The rooftop terrace with pool affords fabulous views over the old town. The latest in its impressive line-up of restaurants and bars is Matsuhisa – the only restaurant in Germany to be headed up by internationally celebrated Japanese chef, Nobu Matsuhisa.

Sofitel Munich Bayerpost
MAP K3 ■ Bayerstraße 12 ■ (089) 599480 ■ www.sofitel.com ■ €€€
This five-star hotel has been created behind the historic façade of a Wilhelmine post office building and offers a contemporary and elegant setting for banquets or conferences. The extensive spa area, well-equipped gym and an exclusive restaurant all combine to make a stay at this hotel a truly luxurious experience.

Hotel Vier Jahreszeiten Kempinski
MAP N3 ■ Maximilianstr. 17 ■ (089) 21250 ■ www.kempinski.com ■ €€€
The 316 air-conditioned rooms and suites in this hotel simply ooze elegance and luxury. The Schwarzreiter restaurant – named after Ludwig II's favourite fish dish of deepwater char – offers modern Bavarian cuisine. Wellness area available.

Business Hotels

Hilton Munich City
MAP Q5 ■ Rosenheimer Straße 15 ■ (089) 48040 ■ Limited DA ■ www.hilton.de ■ €€
Offering well-appointed rooms and suites, this hotel can be found right by the Gasteig cultural centre. Guests can take advantage of seven bright and airy meeting rooms with variable seating options, as well as a large ballroom, ideal for hosting events. It also has two restaurants, a bar and café, and a gym.

IntercityHotel München
MAP L3 ■ Bayerstraße 10 ■ (0) 444440 ■ www.intercityhotel.de ■ Limited DA ■ €€
This hotel is right by the Hauptbahnhof and offers a comfortable, sound-proofed rooms. Free Wi-Fi is available in the seven meeting rooms and in the guest rooms. There's also a restaurant and bar.

Mövenpick Hotel München-Airport
Ludwigstraße 43, Hallbergmoos ■ (0) 811 8880 ■ www.moevenpick.com ■ Limited DA ■ €€
This state-of-the-art, four-star conference hotel can be found just a few minutes away from Munich Airport. It offers comfortable, sound-proofed rooms complete with Wi-Fi, as well as ten conference rooms. There is aso a restaurant and a beer garden in which to unwind, serving traditional Bavarian fare.

Marriott Hotel München

MAP G1 ■ Berliner Straße 93 ■ (089) 360020 ■ www.marriott.de ■ Limited DA ■ €€–€€€

This functional and convenient hotel with 348 rooms and suites has tech-enabled conference rooms and a business center, making it the ideal choice for business travellers. There is also a pool and a spa, perfect for unwinding at the end of a long day.

Hilton Munich Airport Hotel

Terminalstraße Mitte 20, Oberding ■ (089) 97820 ■ Limited DA ■ www.hilton-munich-airport.hoteles-munich.com ■ €€€

The main attraction of this hotel is its impressive atrium, lined with 20-m (65-ft) high palm trees and with an unobstructed view of the runway – an ideal backdrop for receptions, exhibitions and presentations. The spacious bedrooms are furnished to the highest standard. It also has a business centre, spa and wellness area, and a gym. Breakfast is not included.

Mid-Range Hotels

Hotel Europäischer Hof

MAP L3 ■ Bayerstraße 31 ■ (089) 551510 ■ www.heh.de ■ €–€€

This three-star hotel is located opposite the Hauptbahnhof. There's a breakfast buffet, handy underground parking and special deals for children. Pets are welcome. All rooms have Internet access, and there's also a meeting room available.

Hotel Seibel

MAP J4 ■ Theresienhöhe 9 ■ (089) 5 401420 ■ www.seibel-hotels-munich.de ■ €–€€

This three-star, Art Nouveau hotel offers 50 comfortable rooms (including triples and quads) with free Wi-Fi. Some rooms have a balcony overlooking Theresienwiese. There are special rates for same-day bookings.

Hotel Admiral

MAP N5 ■ Kohlstraße 9 ■ (089) 216350 ■ www.hotel-admiral.de ■ €€

This four-star hotel opposite the Deutsches Museum has 32 cosy, individually styled rooms and beautiful gardens that create a relaxing atmosphere. Pets are welcome, and limited smoking rooms are available. There is an organic breakfast buffet.

Alpen Hotel München

MAP L3 ■ Adolf-Kolping-Straße 14 ■ (089) 559330 ■ www.alpenhotel-muenchen.de ■ Limited DA ■ €€

Conveniently located on a side street, this hotel is close to the pedestrian zone without being noisy. The 55 four-star rooms and junior suites all have Wi-Fi. The menu at its in-house restaurant, Stefan, offers a combination of Bavarian and Mediterranean cooking, and there is also a beautiful courtyard garden to relax in.

Eurostars Grand Central

MAP J2 ■ Arnulfstraße 35 ■ (089) 5 165740 ■ www.eurostarsgrandcentral.com ■ €€

Offering all the latest technical innovations, this hotel has 229 double rooms, 15 triples, eight suites and ten apartments for longer stays. There's also a pool, sauna, sun terrace and Tapas restaurant.

Hotel Herzog

MAP L5 ■ Häberlstraße 9 ■ (089) 59 993901 ■ www.hotel-herzog-muenchen.com ■ €€

Eighty stylish and comfortable rooms await guests at this hotel, which is conveniently located next to the Goetheplatz U-Bahn station. Most rooms have their own balcony with a view over the idyllic inner courtyard garden. Breakfast is not included.

Hotel Ibis München City Arnulfpark

MAP J2 ■ Arnulfstraße 55 ■ (089) 2 324930 ■ www.ibis.com ■ Limited DA ■ €€

A member of the Accor Group, this hotel offers 204 air-conditioned rooms (including ten rooms for guests with special access requirements) and is located a stone's throw from the Hauptbahnhof. Offers easy access to the city centre – the tram stop is right outside.

Leonardo Hotel

MAP L3 ■ Senefelder-straße 4 ■ (089) 551540 ■ www.leonardo-hotels.com ■ €€

A quietly situated hotel close to the Hauptbahn-hof, offering 80 modern rooms with free Wi-Fi. Serves an organic breakfast. There is parking, although it is subject to a charge.

Hotel Leopold
MAP G2 ▪ **Leopoldstr. 119** ▪ (089) 367061 ▪ www.hotel-leopold.de ▪ **Limited wheelchair access** ▪ €€

The classic style and idyllic garden at this traditional hotel in the heart of Schwabing, reflect the efforts of a family-run operation. All 100 rooms offer four-star comfort. Special beds for allergy sufferers are available on request.

Arthotel Munich
MAP K3 ▪ **Paul-Heyse-Straße 10** ▪ (089) 592122 ▪ www.arthotelmunich.com ▪ €€–€€€

Occupying a beautiful, centrally located Art Nouveau building, the Arthotel is stylishly appointed throughout. It is convenient for all forms of public transport. Parking is available within the building.

Hotels with Flair

Angelo by Vienna House
MAP H6 ▪ **Leuchtenberg-gring 20** ▪ (089) 1 890860 ▪ **Limited DA** ▪ www.viennahouse.com ▪ €€

The hallmark of this hotel is its vibrant colour scheme. There are two meeting rooms, a business centre and a jazz bar on site. There's also free Wi-Fi in rooms.

Design Hotel Stadt Rosenheim
MAP R5 ▪ **Orleansplatz 6A** ▪ (089) 4 482424 ▪ www.hotel-stadt-rosenheim.de ▪ €€

Every room in this hotel dating back to 1890 is unique. The beds have orthopaedic mattresses

for a great night's sleep. Offers a superb breakfast with free-range eggs.

Anna Hotel
MAP L3 ▪ **Schützenstraße 1** ▪ (089) 599940 ▪ www.annahotel.de ▪ €€–€€€

This boutique hotel – a gem in an ideal location – is run by the Geisel family, renowned hoteliers in Munich (Hotel Königshof and Excelsior are also theirs). A popular feature is the contemporary in-house restaurant/bar.

Cortiina Hotel
MAP N4 ▪ **Ledererstraße 8** ▪ (089) 2 422490 ▪ www.cortiina.com ▪ €€–€€€

A stylish city hotel with an individual style. The interiors of the 33 rooms are finished with natural wood and stone, linen and leather. The bar is a fashionable destination for cocktails.

H'Otello
MAP N4 ▪ **Baaderstraße 1** ▪ (089) 45 831200 ▪ www.hotello.de/b01-muenchen ▪ €€–€€€

The perfect choice for design purists, the H'Otello is a sophisticated hotel located near the Isartor. Its impressive rooftop terrace provides an incredible view of the city centre, and its central location makes it ideal for shopping and sightseeing.

Flushing Meadows
MAP M5 ▪ **Fraunhofer-straße 32** ▪ (089) 55 279170 ▪ flushing meadowshotel.com ▪ €€€

Located on the top two floors of an industrial building, this trendy designer hotel in the city's Glockenbach quarter

offers loft studios and penthouses complete with terraces. Popular rooftop bar. Bike hire is also available at no extra cost.

Budget Hotels

Hotel Dolomit
MAP L3 ▪ **Goethestraße 11** ▪ (089) 592847 ▪ www.hotel-dolomit.de ▪ €

This affordable two-star hotel is located close to the Hauptbahnhof and Theresienwiese. Its 91 rooms (including triples) have soundproofed windows and Wi-Fi. Meeting rooms are available. Breakfast is not included.

Hotel Garni Lex im Gartenhof
MAP L2 ▪ **Brienner Straße 48** ▪ (089) 5 427260 ▪ www.hotel-lex.de ▪ €

Situated in a secluded courtyard, this friendly hotel with simple yet modern rooms is the only hotel in the museum quarter where the museums are all within walking distance. Apartments are available for longer-term stays.

Motel One München-Sendlinger Tor
MAP M4 ▪ **Herzog-Wilhelm-Straße 28** ▪ (089) 51 77 72 50 ▪ **Limited DA** ▪ www.motel-one.com ▪ €

This budget hotel with a designer twist is a real gem. The "Sendlinger Tor" building can be found right in the heart of the old town, and plenty of attractions are located within walking distance. There is free Wi-Fi but breakfast is not included.

Hotel Royal

MAP L3 ■ Schillerstraße 11a ■ (089) 59 988160 ■ www.hotel-royal.de ■ €
This centrally located three-star hotel has 40 non-smoking rooms with soundproofed windows. Family and shared rooms are available and there is free Wi-Fi.

Hotel Blauer Bock

MAP M3 ■ Sebastiansplatz 9 ■ (089) 231780 ■ www.hotel blauerbock.de ■ €–€€
This family-run hotel is right next to Viktualienmarkt. The 400-year-old house is brimming with old-world Munich charm and also incorporates a traditional restaurant of the same name. Parking is available.

Hostels, B&Bs and Apartments

Bed & Breakfast München

■ www.bedandbreakfast.de/muenchen ■ €
This company offers an alternative to hotel rooms, namely guest rooms and apartments with or without breakfast for stays from one night to weeks or even months.

Concept Living Munich

■ Pfälzer-Wald-Straße 2 ■ (089) 66 008910 ■ www.concept-living-munich.de ■ €
Seven apartment-style spaces, located in the Giesing quarter, are available for one to eight people. Offering modern decor and furnishings with a kitchen and bathroom, and facilities including a DVD player and Internet access.

Euro Youth Hotel Munich

MAP L3 ■ Senefelderstraße 5 ■ (089) 5 990880 ■ www.euro-youth-hotel.de ■ €
The bedrooms and dorms at this centrally located hostel are wonderfully bright and roomy. Wi-Fi is available, and breakfast is included with single and double rooms. There is a Euro bar with live music at weekends, and happy hour is from 5:30 to 9pm.

Jaeger's Hostel

MAP L3 ■ Senefelderstraße 3 ■ (089) 555281 ■ www.jaegershotel.de ■ €
This colourful hostel, located a stone's throw from Munich Central Station, offers the full range of room types from dorms through to singles with en-suite bathrooms. There is free Wi-Fi and a bar on site.

Smart Stay Hostel Munich City

MAP L4 ■ Mozartstraße 4 ■ (089) 558 7970 ■ Limited DA ■ www.munichcity.smart-stay.de ■ €
This hostel near Goetheplatz (which has a sister building at Schützenstraße 7) offers single and double rooms with bathrooms, as well as dorms. Additional features include a bar, restaurant, small self-service kitchen and bicycle hire.

Wombat's City Hostel Munich

MAP L3 ■ Senefelderstraße 1 ■ (089) 5998 9180 ■ Limited DA ■ www.wombats-hostels.com ■ €
This hostel near the Hauptbahnhof offers a combination of dorms and double bedrooms – all with showers and lockers. There is also a glass-roofed courtyard brimming with plants. Free Wi-Fi.

Frederics Serviced Apartments

(089) 45 243895 ■ www.frederics.eu/de ■ €€
City apartments with separate living and sleeping areas are available at three different locations within Munich (by the Olympiapark, Hohenzollernplatz or the Englischer Garten). For those enjoying longer stays, the apartment is cleaned and bedlinen and towels changed once a week. Guests can book additional services as required.

Maximilian Munich Apartments & Hotel

MAP N4 ■ Hochbrückenstraße 18 ■ (089) 242580 ■ www.maximilian-munich.com ■ €€€
Accommodation options here include 54 studios, suites and apartments in the main building and two summer houses in the rose garden. All of the options come complete with a sleeping and living area. There's also a restaurant and bar.

Mr. Lodge

(089) 340 8230 ■ www.mrlodge.de ■ €€€
Mr. Lodge offers a wide range of accommodation options from furnished one-bedroom apartments to four-bedroom houses, as well as exclusive business suites. Website updated daily.

For a key to hotel price categories see p148

General Index

Acknowledgments

Author

Dr Elfi Ledig has worked for many years as an author and editor of reference books and travel guides. She is currently Editor-in-Chief of a Munich health and wellness magazine and lives in Munich.

Publishing Director Georgina Dee

Publisher Vivien Antwi

Design Director Phil Ormerod

Editorial Kate Berens, Alice Fewery, Rachel Fox, Petra Zanner

Design Ute Berretz, Tessa Bindloss, Marisa Renzullo, Priyanka Thakur

Commissioned Photography Dorota Jarymowicz/Mariusz Jarymowicz; Lynne McPeake, William Reavell, Rough Guides/Demetrio Carrasco, William Shaw, Roger Smith, Angela Stacey, Stuart West.

Picture Research Ellen Root

Cartography Casper Morris

DTP Jason Little

Production Igrain Roberts

Factchecker Marc di Duca

Proofreader Clare Peel

Indexer Hilary Bird

Illustrator Matthias Liesendahl

Translation Andiamo! Language Services

Picture Credits

The publisher would like to thank the following for their kind permission to reproduce their photographs:
Key: a-above; b-below/bottom; c-centre; f-far; l-left; r-right; t-top

Alamy Stock Photo: age fotostock / Howard Stapleton 108cla; ALLTRAVEL / Peter Mross 4cla; Arcaid Images / Nigel Young / Foster & Partners 97tl; Bildarchiv Monheim GmbH / Florian Monheim 106tl; Timo Christ 34-5; DanitaDelimont.com / Martin Zwick 90tl; dpa picture alliance Archive / Frank Leonhardt 62b; filmfoto-03edit 75cl; Peter Forsberg 22crb; Dennis Hallinan 96cla; imageBROKER / Günter Lenz 53cl, / Manfred Bail 100tl, / Martin Siepmann 22-3, / Petra Wallner 106crb; INTERFOTO 40clb, 42cb, Schloss Nymphenburg *Lola Montez* (1847) by J.K. Stieler 30cl, Munich City Museum/ *After the assassination of Kurt Eisner February 21st 1919 in Munich* by Emanuel Bachrach-Baré 41cla; Andrew Michael 31crb; OnTheRoad 35cr; Prisma by Dukas Presseagentur GmbH 44br; Prochasson Frederic 103t; Sueddeutsche Zeitung Photo 51cl; Sueddeutsche Zeitung Photo / Stephan Rump 109tl; traveler 46t; Steve Vidler 112tl; Westend61 GmbH / Martin Siepmann 74br; **Allianz Arena:** B. Ducke 70bl.
Artothek: Alte Pinakothek, Munich *Battle of Alexander at Issus* (1529) by Albrecht Altdorfer 18bc, *Land of Cockaigne* (1566) by Pieter Brueghel 18c, *Disrobing of Christ* (c.1608) by El Greco 19clb, *Willem van Heythuysen* (c.1625) by Frans Hals 19tl, *The Rape of the Daughters of Leucippus* (1618) by Peter Paul Rubens photo Blauel/Gnamm 19cra; Neue Pinakothek *Neptune's Horses* (1892) by Walter Cranes 20t, *Breakfast in the Studio* (1868) by Édouard Manet 20clb, *Still Life: Vase with Twelve Sunflowers* (1881) by Vincent Van Gogh 98br.
AWL Images: Walter Bibikow 79tr; Cahir Davitt 72b.

Bavaria Filmstadt 2016: 54t. **Bayerische Staatsoper:** Wilfried Hösl *Alice Im Wunderland*-Choreographie Christopher Wheeldon, Musik Joby Talbot, Musikalische Leitung Myron Romanul 75tr. **Bayerische Verwaltung der Staatlichen Schlösser, Gärten und Seen:** 36cr, 36bl, 37cr; Dorling Kindersley/ Dorota Jarymowicz, Mariusz Jarymowicz 16bl, 17crb, 134clb. **Bob Beaman:** 56b. **Blutsgeschwister GmbH:** 69clb, 85cl. **BMW AG:** 32cl, 129cl. **Boulderwelt:** Tobias Leipnitz 70t.

Café Lotti: 63clb

Deutsche Eiche: 57br. **Deutsches Museum:** S. Wameser 26cla, 26crb, 27tl, 28tr, 28bl, 29cl, 29b, 50tr, 119tr. **Doppler Shop:** Sabine Doppler 115bc. **Dreamstime.com:** Acrogame 65cla; Anderm 48b; Annemario 47clb; Beriliu 17tl; Cyphix 89b; Danbreckwoldt 15cr; Electropower 12bl; Elenatur 37tl, 135b; Fottoo 23tl, 104tl; Gordzam 11tl, Mapics 3tl, 76-7; Matewe 46bl; Patrickwang 128br; Paulmz 64br; Rosshelen l 95clb; Rudi1976 2tl, 8-9; Whosegallery 132c; Yfwong74 16c; Zoom-zoom 4cra.

Erzbischofliches Odinariat Munich: Dorling Kindersley/Pawel Wojcik 41tr. **EurArt:** 73tl.

FC Bayern Basketball: 120tr. **Ferdings GmbH:** Stefan Herx 123crb. **Filmfest München:** 54bl. **Flushing Meadows:** 62tr. **Stefanie Franz:** 1, 2tr, 3tr, 4clb, 4b, 6cla, 7tl, 7cra, 10cr, 10clb, 10br, 11ca, 12cl, 12-3, 13cra, 14cra, 14clb, 14br, 14-5, 15tr, 17cl, 18tr, 22bl, 24-5, 26tr, 30clb, 30-1, 38-9, 40tc, 42t, 43bl, 44t, 49crb, 55tr, 58c, 58br, 63br, 64tl, 64c, 66tl, 66c, 66br, 67br, 68tr, 72cla, 73br, 82clb, 83cra, 84br, 86-7, 89tr, 90b, 92tl, 92bc, 93tl, 93crb, 97b, 98t, 99cl, 100br, 101cla, 101clb, 103br, 104bl, 105cl, 107cl, 107br, 108br, 111br, 112bl, 113cl,114tl, 114br, 116cla, 117cb, 121cl, 124tr, 124crb, 127cr, 130br, 136t, 138–9.

Gärtnerplatztheater: Ida Zenna 4t; Anton Brandl 81cl. **Gasteig:** 52t . **Vera Gaudermann:** 69tr. **Geisel Privathotels:** Thomas Haberland 61cl. **Getty Images:** Hannes Magerstaedt 128tl. **Green City e.V:** Gleb Polovnykov 74cla.

HOFSTATT: 68bl, 85tr.

iStockphoto.com: Bankbuster 78cl; benedek 79bl.

Jüdisches Museum München: Roland Halbe 80tl.

Kindermuseum München: 50clb. **Kino am Olympiasee:** 32br, 55cl. **Kokolores:** Katrin Göbel 115tr.

La Kaz: 125b. **Livingroom:** Gerals Klepka 115cl. **Lollo Rosso:** 116br. **Löwenbräukeller:** Kerstin Jungblut 67cla.

Metropoltheater: Jakob Piloty 53tr. **Milch und Bar:** 84tl. **MÜNCHEN MARATHON:** Norbert Wilhelmi 71tr. **Münchner Stadtmuseum:** 80bc. **Museum Fu ünf Kontinente:** 43tr, 112cb.

Olympiapark München: 4crb, 11cb, 32–3, 41bl.

Pinakothek der Moderne: Anton Brandl 21bl. **Prinz Myshkin:** 59tc, 59br, 83bl. **Julian Puttins:** 11clb, 34clb, 35tl.

Residenz Theater: Thomas Aurin 52bl. **Restaurant Tantris:** Christoph A. Hellhake 60bl. **Rote Sonne:** Südmotor GmbH, Bernd Bergmann/Christoph Ziegler 57cl. **Ruffini:** 131cr.

Sai Spa: Peter Hinze 71cl. **Sea Life:** 33tr, 120cl. **Stadtwerke München:** Kerstin Groh 33crb, 130tl. **Stereo Café:** 94t. **Strom:** 56tl.

Dr. Jörg Theilacker: 118cra, 120bl, 122tr, 122br. **Tourist-Information Bad Tölz:** 65br.

Volkssternwarte München: 48tl.

White Rabbit's Room: 61tr.

Zauberberg: Claudia Kimbacher 60tr. **Zuckertag:** 51tr.

Cover

Front and spine: **Getty Images:** Westend61.

Back: **Dreamstime.com:** Noppasin Wongchum.

Pull Out Map Cover

Getty Images: Westend61

All other images © Dorling Kindersley
For further information see: www.dkimages.com

As a guide to abbreviations in visitor information blocks: **Adm** *= admission charge;* **DA** *= disabled access;* **D** *= dinner;* **L** *= lunch.*

Printed and bound in China

First American Edition 2005
Published in the United States by
DK Publishing, 345 Hudson Street,
New York, New York 10014

Copyright 2005, 2017 © Dorling
Kindersley Limited

A Penguin Random House Company

17 18 19 20 10 9 8 7 6 5 4 3 2 1

**Reprinted with revisions 2007, 2009,
2011, 2013, 2015, 2017**

Published in Great Britain by Dorling
Kindersley Limited.

A catalog record for this book is available
from the Library of Congress.

ISSN 1479-344X
ISBN 978 1 4654 6780 5

MIX
Paper from
responsible sources
FSC™ C018179

Phrase Book

In an Emergency

Where is the telephone?	Wo ist das Telefon?	voh ist duss tel-e-fon?
Help!	Hilfe!	hilf-uh
Please call a doctor	Bitte rufen Sie einen Arzt	bitt-uh roof'n zee ine-en artst
Please call the police	Bitte rufen Sie die Polizei	bitt-uh roof'n zee dee poli-tsy
Please call the fire brigade	Bitte rufen Sie die Feuerwehr	bitt-uh roof'n zee dee foyer-vayr
Stop!	Halt!	hult

Communication Essentials

Yes	Ja	yah
No	Nein	nine
Please	Bitte	bitt-uh
Thank you	Danke	dunk-uh
Excuse me	Verzeihung	fair-tsy-hoong
Hello (good day)	Guten Tag	goot-en tahk
Hello	Grüß Gott	grooss got
Goodbye	Auf Wiedersehen	owf-veed-er-zay-ern
Good evening	Guten Abend	goot'n ahb'nt
Good night	Gute Nacht	goot-uh nukht
Until tomorrow	Bis morgen	biss morg'n
See you	Tschüss	chooss
See you	Servus	sayr voos
What is that?	Was ist das?	voss ist duss
Why?	Warum?	var-room
Where?	Wo?	voh
When?	Wann?	vunn
today	heute	hoyt-uh
tomorrow	morgen	morg'n
month	Monat	mohn-aht
night	Nacht	nukht
afternoon	Nachmittag	nahkh-mit-tahk
morning	Morgen	morg'n
year	Jahr	yui
there	dort	dort
here	hier	hear
week	Woche	vokh-uh
yesterday	gestern	gest'n
evening	Abend	ahb'nt

Useful Phrases

How are you? (informal)	Wie geht's?	vee gayts
Fine, thanks	Danke, es geht mir gut	dunk-uh, es gayt meer goot
Until later	Bis später	biss shpay-ter
Where is/are..?	Wo ist/sind...?	voh ist/sind
How far is it to...?	Wie weit ist es...?	vee vite ist ess
Do you speak English?	Sprechen Sie Englisch?	shpresh'n zee eng-glish
I don't understand	Ich verstehe nicht	ish fair-shtay-uh nisht
Could you speak more slowly?	Könnten Sie langsamer sprechen?	kurnt-en zee lung-zam-er shpresh'n

Useful Words

large	groß	grohss
small	klein	kline
hot	heiß	hyce
cold	kalt	kult
good	gut	goot
bad	böse/schlecht	burss-uh/shlesht
open	geöffnet	g'urff-nett
closed	geschlossen	g'shloss'n
left	links	links
right	rechts	reshts
straight ahead	geradeaus	g'rah-der-owss

Making a Telephone Call

I would like to make a phone call	Ich möchte telefonieren	ish mer-shtuh tel-e-fon-eer'n
I'll try again later	Ich versuche es später noch einmal	ish fair-zookh-uh es shpay-ter nokh ine-mull
Can I leave a message?	Kann ich eine Nachricht hinterlassen?	kan ish ine-uh nakh-risht hint-er-lahss-en
answerphone	Anrufbeantworter	an-roof-be-ahnt-vort-er
telephone card	Telefonkarte	tel-e-fohn-kart-uh
receiver	Hörer	hur-er
mobile	Handy	han-dee
engaged (busy)	besetzt	b'zetst
wrong number	falsche Verbindung	falsh-uh fair-bin-doong

Sightseeing

entrance ticket	Eintrittskarte	ine-tritz-kart-uh
cemetery	Friedhof	freed-hofe
train station	Bahnhof	barn-hofe
gallery	Galerie	gall-er-ree
information	Auskunft	owss-koonft
church	Kirche	keersh-uh
garden	Garten	gart'n
palace/castle	Palast/Schloss	pall-ast/shloss
place (square)	Platz	plats
bus stop	Haltestelle	hal-te-shtel-uh
free admission	Eintritt frei	ine-tritt fry

Shopping

Do you have/ Is there..?	Gibt es...?	geept ess
How much does it cost?	Was kostet das?	voss kost't duss?
When do you open/ close?	Wann öffnen Sie? schließen Sie?	vunn off'n zee shlees'n zee
this	das	duss
expensive	teuer	toy-er
cheap	preiswert	price-vurt
size	Größe	gruhs-uh
number	Nummer	noom-er
colour	Farbe	farb-uh
brown	braun	brown
black	schwarz	shvarts
red	rot	roht
blue	blau	blau
green	grün	groon
yellow	gelb	gelp

Types of Shop

chemist (pharmacy)	Apotheke	appo-tay-kuh
bank	Bank	bunk
market	Markt	markt
travel agency	Reisebüro	rye-zer-boo-roe
department store	Warenhaus	vahr'n-hows
chemist's, drugstore	Drogerie	droog-er-ree
hairdresser	Friseur	freezz-er
newspaper kiosk	Zeitungskiosk	tsytoongs-kee-osk
bookshop	Buchhandlung	bookh-hant-loong
bakery	Bäckerei	beck-er-eye
butcher	Metzgerei	mets-ger-eye
post office	Post	posst
shop/store	Geschäft/Laden	gush-eft/lard'n
photography shop	Photogeschäft	fo-to-gush-eft
clothes shop	Kleiderladen, Boutique	kly-der-lard'n, boo-teek-uh

Staying in a Hotel

Do you have any vacancies?	Haben Sie noch Zimmer frei?	harb'n zee nokh tsimm-er-fry
with twin beds?	mit zwei Betten?	mitt tsvy bett'n
with a double bed?	mit einem Doppelbett?	mitt ine'm dopp'l-bet
with a bath?	mit Bad?	mitt bart
with a shower?	mit Dusche?	mitt doosh-uh
I have a reservation	Ich habe eine Reservierung	ish harb-uh ine-uh rez-er-veer-oong
key	Schlüssel	shlooss'l
porter	Pförtner	pfert-ner

Eating Out

Do you have a table for...?	Haben Sie einen Tisch für...?	harb'n zee tish foor
I would like to reserve a table	Ich möchte eine Reservierung machen	ish mer-shtuh ine-uh rezer-veer-oong makh'n
I'm a vegetarian	Ich bin Vegetarier	ish bin vegg-er-tah-ree-er
Waiter!	Herr Ober!	hair oh-bare!
The bill (check), please	Die Rechnung, bitte	dee resh-noong bitt-uh
breakfast	Frühstück	froo-shtock
lunch	Mittagessen	mit-targ-ess'n
dinner	Abendessen	arb'nt-ess'n
bottle	Flasche	flush-uh
dish of the day	Tagesgericht	tahg-es-gur-isht
main dish	Hauptgericht	howpt-gur-isht
dessert	Nachtisch	nahkh-tish
cup	Tasse	tass-uh
wine list	Weinkarte	vine-kart-uh
glass	Glas	glars
spoon	Löffel	lerff'l
fork	Gabel	gahb'l
teaspoon	Teelöffel	tay-lerff'l
knife	Messer	mess-er
starter (appetizer)	Vorspeise	for-shpize-uh
the bill	Rechnung	resh-noong
tip	Trinkgeld	trink-gelt
plate	Teller	tell-er

Menu Decoder

Apfel	upf'l	apple
Apfelsine	upf'l-seen-uh	orange
Aprikose	upri-kawz-uh	apricot
Artischocke	arti-shokh-uh	artichoke
Aubergine	or-ber-jeen-uh	aubergine (eggplant)
Banane	bar-narn-uh	banana
Beefsteak	beef-stayk	steak
Bier	beer	beer
Bohnensuppe	burn-en-zoop-uh	bean soup
Bratkartoffeln	brat-kar-toff'l'n	fried potatoes
Bratwurst	brat-voorst	fried sausage
Brezel	bret-sell	pretzel
Brot	brot	bread
Brühe	bruh-uh	broth
Butter	boot-ter	butter
Champignon	shum-pin-yong	mushroom
Currywurst	kha-ree-voorst	sausage with curry sauce
Ei	eye	egg
Eis	ice	ice/ ice cream
Ente	ent-uh	duck
Erdbeeren	ayrt-beer'n	strawberries
Fisch	fish	fish
Fleisch	flysh	meat
Forelle	for-ell-uh	trout
Gans	ganns	goose
gebraten	g'braat'n	fried
Geflügel	g'floog'l	poultry
gegrillt	g'grilt	grilled
gekocht	g'kokht	boiled
Gemüse	g'mooz-uh	vegetables
geräuchert	g'rowk-ert	smoked
Gulasch	goo-lush	goulash

Hähnchen (Hendl)	haynsh'n	chicken
Hering	hair-ing	herring
Himbeeren	him-beer'n	raspberries
Kaffee	kaf-fay	coffee
Kalbfleisch	kalp-flysh	veal
Kaninchen	ka-neensh'n	rabbit
Karotte	car-ott-uh	carrot
Kartoffelpüree	kar-toff'l-poor-ay	mashed potatoes
Käse	kayz-uh	cheese
Knoblauch	k'nob-lowkh	garlic
Knödel	k'nerd'l	dumpling
Kuchen	kookh'n	cake
Lachs	lahkhs	salmon
Leber	lay-ber	liver
Marmelade	marmer-lard-uh	marmalade, jam
Milch	milsh	milk
Mineralwasser	minn-er-arl vuss-er	mineral water
Nuss	nooss	nut
Öl	erl	oil
Olive	o-leev-uh	olive
Pfeffer	pfeff-er	pepper
Pfirsich	pfir-sh	peach
Pflaume	pflow-me	plum
Pommes frites	pomm-fritt	chips/ French fries
Rindfleisch	rint-flysh	beef
Rührei	rhoo-er-eye	scrambled eggs
Saft	zuft	juice
Salat	zal-aat	salad
Salz	zults	salt
Sauerkirschen	zow-er-keersh'n	cherries
Sauerkraut	zow-er-krowt	sauerkraut
Sekt	zekt	sparkling wine
Senf	zenf	mustard
scharf	sharf	spicy
Schlagsahne	shlahgg-zarn-uh	whipped cream
Schnitzel	shnitz'l	veal or pork cutlet
Schweinefleisch	shvine-flysh	pork
Semmel	tsem-mel	bread roll
Spargel	shparg'l	asparagus
Spiegelei	shpeeg'l-eye	fried egg
Spinat	shpin-art	spinach
Tee	tay	tea
Tomate	tom-art-uh	tomato
Wassermelone	vuss-er-me-lohn-uh	watermelon
Wein	vine	wine
Weintrauben	vine-trowb'n	grapes
Wiener	veen-er	frankfurter
Würstchen	voorst-sh'n	
Zitrone	tsi-trohn-uh	lemon
Zucker	tsook-er	sugar
Zwiebel	tsveeb'l	onion

Numbers

0	null	nool
1	eins	eye'ns
2	zwei	tsvy
3	drei	dry
4	vier	feer
5	fünf	foonf
6	sechs	zex
7	sieben	zeeb'n
8	acht	uhkht
9	neun	noyn
10	zehn	tsayn
11	elf	elf
12	zwölf	tsverlf
13	dreizehn	dry-tsayn
14	vierzehn	feer-tsayn
15	fünfzehn	foonf-tsayn
16	sechzehn	zex-tsayn
17	siebzehn	zeep-tsayn
18	achtzehn	uhkht-tsayn
19	neunzehn	noyn-tsayn
20	zwanzig	tsvunn-tsig

Street Index